W9-ATH-254

Archaeological Discoveries
Relative to the Judaeo-Christians

PUBLICATIONS OF THE STUDIUM BIBLICUM FRANCISCANUM

Collectio minor No. 10

ARCHAEOLOGICAL DISCOVERIES

RELATIVE TO THE JUDAEO - CHRISTIANS

Historical Survey

by

Ignazio Mancini, o.f.m.

ST. JOSEPH'S UNIVERSITY   STX

BR131.M2413
Archaeological discoveries relative to t

3 9353 00163 2874

BR
131
,M2413

FRANCISCAN PRINTING PRESS
JERUSALEM
1970

164990

VI

Original title of the work:
"Le Scoperte Archeologiche sui Giudeo-Cristiani—Note storiche"
Collectio assisiensis n. 6, Studio Teologico Porziuncola.
Assisi, 1968.
Translation by G. Bushell, updated by the author.

Cum permissu superiorum

All rights reserved

2256-XI-70

CONTENTS

ABBREVIATIONS

The following symbols are normally used in abbreviation of the titles of the respective works:

LA   =   *Studii Biblici Franciscani Liber Annuus*. Jerusalem.
Studium Biblicum Franciscanum.

RB   =   *Revue Biblique*. Jérusalem. L'Ecole archéologique et biblique française.

LTS   =   *La Terra Santa* (Italian edition). Franciscan Press, Jerusalem.

GSDF =   *Gli scavi del 'Dominus Flevit' (Monte Oliveto - Gerusalemme). Parte I: La necropoli del periodo romano* in collaborazione con J. T. Milik per le iscrizioni. Gerusalemme, 1958.

ISGC =   *Il simbolismo dei Giudeo-cristiani*. Gerusalemme, 1962.

LEC =   *L'Eglise de la Circoncision*. Traduction d'A. Storme, d'après le manuscrit italien. Jérusalem, 1965.

LHF =   *L'Huile de la Foi*. L'Onction des malades sur une lamelle du Ier siècle. Traduit et adapté de l'Italien par O. Englebert. Jérusalem, 1967.

PG   =   Migne *Patrologia Graeca*.

PL   =   Migne *Patrologia Latina*.

PREFACE

Why should we be writing a history of the archaeological discoveries relative to primitive Jewish Christianity? This is a question which may occur to many. I think it calls for a prompt answer and, perhaps, in the light of this, the purpose of the present book will be more clearly seen.

The warm welcome which scholars gave my article, "Ecclesia ex circumcisione" [1] treating briefly of discoveries and research relative to early Jewish Christianity has encouraged me to deal with the subject again and on a fuller scale.

I am also convinced that what is said hereinafter will aid scholars to get a fuller picture of the recent finds which have thrown so much light on early Jewish Christianity. A description of the attendant circumstances of time, place, method, and a knowledge of main personalities who have contributed, some quite consciously, some in a material fashion, will surely help considerably towards a more complete appreciation of the subject matter and the conclusions involved in this field of research.

There is no need to stress the urge — quite marked in our own days — to rediscover past values now forgotten or hitherto unknown. In the present instance, the subject matter is of general interest since the primitive Church of Jerusalem, like that of other countries in the Near East, is closely bound up with Christian origins.

---

[1] I. Mancini, La "Ecclesia ex circumcisione" in Bibbia e Oriente 7 (1965), pp. 77-87.

12

Though neither archaeologist nor Bible specialist, the writer feels free to deal with the subject because he has lived for many years in the very land of Palestine, observing this development in research and having frequent contact with specialists in the field. The result is that he has gained a knowledge of various facts and circumstances which, it is thought, will be useful to scholars and especially for those who do not live in the Holy Land.

With regard to the evaluation of these studies, I have taken note only of what the specialists have put forward in their publications or in personal contact with me. There may be gaps or omissions. For that I can only plead as excuse the fact that Jerusalem is, at present, somewhat off the beaten paths.

I do not intend to engage in polemics. I propose simply to record the facts, together with the assessment made by others regarding recent studies and discussions on the existence and the structure of the primitive Jewish Christian Church, leaving the reader free to make an objective examination and a personal appraisal.

Throughout the book, I shall follow the chronological order of the discoveries adding, at the same time, the essential bibliography. For the benefit of those competent to judge, I shall also note the reactions of different scholars, sometimes quite diverse in character.

I express my thanks to the professors of the Franciscan House of Biblical Studies, Jerusalem, for allowing me free access to the documents on which the present work is largely based.

Fr. Ignazio Mancini, O.F.M.

CHAPTER I

FIRST FINDS AND FIRST STUDIES

Studies on Judaeo-Christians have come a long way when they can now deliver conclusions which are no longer disturbing. Voices raised a century ago claiming that some archaeological discoveries in the Holy Land might be relative to a Christian community of pre-Constantine times were lone and shy. Often the opinion was that of some isolated scholar, basing his conclusions on very meagre finds.

Fifty years were to pass before other voices joined those at the beginning and before more abundant material was discovered. The period 1873 to 1953 may be considered the opening one in so far as finds relative to the Jewish Christian Church are concerned. The following are the discoveries made during this long stretch of time: the ossuaries of Bat'n el-Hawa and of Talpiot, the tombs of Sanhedria, funerary lamellae, papyri and other inscriptions.

1. *The Ossuaries of Bat'n el-Hawa.*

The first discoveries of Jewish Christian material which caused a flutter amongst scholars date back about a century. It was in 1873 that an Arab found thirty ossuaries in a room carved out of rock at Bat'n el-Hawa (Mount of Scandal), Jerusalem. The finder mentioned the fact to the noted French scholar Clermont-Ganneau who took notes and made sketches, while his draftsman, A. Lecomte of Noüy, copied the inscriptions adorning the ossuaries.

14

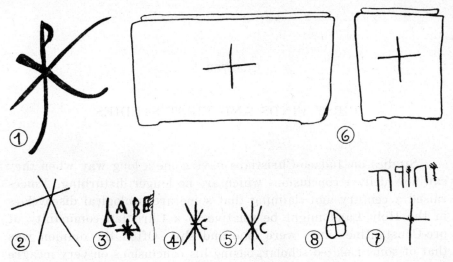

Fig. 1. Signs on the ossuaries of Bat'n el Hawa (No. 2, 7), of Talpiot (No. 6)
and of other sites (1,3,4,5,8) From *LA* III, p. 175

In an initial article,[1] Clermont-Ganneau brought scholars up
to date on some of the discoveries stating that he wished students
to become aware of the contents of such priceless documents. He
was of the opinion that the ossuaries contained the human remains
of more than one generation, and that some of them were indicative
of an evolving Christianity. In the article, the writer promised
further treatment of the subject and, in the event, returned to the
subject in the first volume of his works translated into English
and more profusely illustrated.[2]

1   C. Clermont-Ganneau, "Epigraphes hebraïques et grecques sur des ossuaires
     juifs inédits," in *Revue Archéologique*, troisième série (1883), tome Ier, pp.
     257-268.
2   C. Clermont-Ganneau, *Archaeological Researches in Palestine during the
     Years 1873-1874*. Vol. I. London, 1899, pp. 381-412.

He conceived of a distinction between two groups of Jews :
the faithful belonging to the synagogue, and those who followed
the Cross. He discerned within the one family who owned the tomb
a double current of religious thought, since some members came
to know Christianity and made it their faith.

The reasons which led Clermont-Ganneau to state that some of
the ossuaries in question belonged to Judaeo-Christians are these:

(a) Some proper names had a Christian flavour, e.g. Kyrikos ;
(b) other various symbols, amongst them the X before the name
     of Jesus in Greek, as also the sign of the cross "immissa" ;
(c) a large cross finely chiselled under the name "Jude."

Sensing the surprise which his conclusions would evoke he
wrote, *inter alia*, "The discovery of the presence of Christianity in
an old Jewish family, with its own tomb close to the gates of Jerusalem is, in my opinion. something extraordinary and unprecedented.
In any case, is this sufficient reason for declaring the thing impossible, *a priori?*" [3]

For some scholars interested in Palestiniana, the conclusions
of Clermont-Ganneau were highly satisfactory. The Englishman,
Colonel Claude R. Conder, a Protestant archaeologist, quite competent
in the field of archaeology of that period, wrote a monumental history of Palestine. Speaking of the ossuaries described by Clermont-
Ganneau, he noted the presence of ossuaries with inscriptions in
Greek and also crosses "apparently Christian." He reproduced several
names written on the ossuaries, some of them, as Clermont-Ganneau
had noted, quite familiar from the Gospels : Jesus, Lazarus, Simeon,
Martha, Jude, etc. He concluded, "It is perhaps not improbable that
these Jewish Christian osteophagi held the bones of Ebionites from
the Hauran, anxious to repose in the Holy City." [4]

3   *Idem, op. cit.*, p. 404.
4   C. R. Conder, *Syrian Stone-Lore*. London, 1896, pp. 259-260.

As can be seen, Conder put the problem a little differently from Clermont-Ganneau. The latter spoke of a family tomb for a group that was originally Jewish. Later, the remains of some members who had gone over to Christianity were buried there. Conder, on the other hand, maintained that the tomb belonged to a Jewish Christian community which he identified with the Ebionites.

The hypothesis stated by Clermont-Ganneau and shared by Conder was not, however, followed up. Catholic writers in the Holy City, while acquainted with and highly respectful of the two scholars, did not attempt to probe the problems of the ossuaries found in Jerusalem's immediate neighbourhood, signed with crosses and bearing proper names of New Testament origin, as well as other symbols which were quite clearly Christian. Further examples of such burial places and ossuaries came to light around Jerusalem, but the question never occurred as to whether or not they contained the human remains of Christians. As we all know, it is not easy to change the minds of experts on positions which seem quite soundly fixed. In this case, the almost dogmatically-held view was that it was quite out of the question that Christian remains of pre-Constantine times could be found near Jerusalem.

So, Catholic writers disregarded the discoveries of Clermont-Ganneau and Conder, and this despite the fact that they had before their very eyes other examples of Christian ossuaries, though they dated from a later period.

For example, Dom H. Leclerc, speaking of "Ossuaries," [5] makes a comparison between an ossuary found in Palestine and another discovered in Africa. He writes, "When, in 1873, Clermont-Ganneau suggested a possible relationship between the Jewish ossuaries and those of Christian martyrs, he made another archaeological guess.

---

5   H. Leclercq, "Ossuaries" in *Dictionnaire d'Archéologie chrétienne et de Liturgie*, XIII, I, coll. 25-27.

In 1895, there has been found in Dalaa, a district of Ain-Beida in North Africa, a rectangular casket, 0.126 metres long, 0.14 wide and 0.13 high. It is kept in the Museum of the Louvre." The ossuary in question is adorned with rosettes, like those of Palestine, and offers a Latin inscription which can be interpreted thus: *Memoria Feliciani pa (ssi) III k(alendas) iulias v(otum) l(ibens) s(olvit) e(iscopus)*. The ossuary is that of Saint Felician who was venerated on that day. The author continues: "Judging from the form of the characters and the delicacy of the decoration, the casket and its inscription date not later than the fourth century."

Thus, Leclerq sensed a relationship and a development in the use of ossuaries deriving from Judaism and passed on to Christians, but he did not reach the same conclusions as held in common by Clermont-Ganneau and Conder. They were of the opinion that if not all the ossuaries, at least some of those found in Palestine, could belong to Christians. Much more curious is the fact, however, that Clermont-Ganneau himself, while following the reading of the inscription suggested by Papier, interpreted it differently and did not recognize the Christian origin of the African ossuary. He held it to be Jewish. [6]

Not even Père Vincent could conceive that the ossuaries found at Bat'n el-Hawa could be Christian, though he must have been familiar enough with the writings of Clermont-Ganneau. In fact, in discussing the ossuary found during diggings in preparation for the construction of the Hospital of St. Louis, near the walls of Jerusalem, he spoke of "a stone casket of a type common amongst Jewish ossuaries but unmistakeably of Christian origin by reason of the large cross in relief which adorned the cover." [7] However,

6   C. Clermont-Ganneau, *Recueil d'Archéologie Orientale*, II, Paris, 1898, pp. 78-79.
7   L. -H. Vincent, *Jérusalem de l'Ancien Testament*, I. Paris, 1954, p. 32.

Vincent never went into the problem of the Christian character of ossuaries. Thus, even in 1954, he was still convinced that the ossuaries found by Clermont-Ganneau could only be Jewish.

Père Frey treats of the ossuary on which the name "Jude" is inscribed (no. 1306). He writes, "Clermont-Ganneau holds that the inscription is Christian because of the fact that a cross is delicately chiselled on it. But, in this connection, one can make observations, similar to those in the case of the preceding inscription." In this regard, he held that the supposedly Jewish names traced on only some of these ossuaries exclude the possibility that the others belonged to Christians for "it is only with difficulty that we can grant that some Christians were buried in a Jewish tomb, even though they belonged to the same family" (no. 1305). On the X placed before the name "Jesus" he states, "The name is preceded by a sign which could be a cross. However, the thing is very dubious" (no. 1327). Regarding another cross traced on the wall of the same burial chamber, he says quite simply, without further elaboration, "The inscription has a symbol in the form of a large cross 'immissa' with unequal arms" (no.1325). [8]

Frey's insistence on rejecting the idea of any kind of Christian character in the inscriptions and symbols appears strange indeed. Stranger than his rejection, however, is the way he goes about it. In fact, he gives no reasons whatsoever. For him, the symbols described just have the form of a cross, but they are not really crosses. The reader is left unsatisfied for there is no explanation at all of the nature of the symbols.

8   J. -B. Frey, *Corpus Inscriptionum Iudaicarum*, II. Rome, 1952, nn. 1306, 1305, 1327, 1325.

2. *The ossuaries of Talpiot.*

In September, 1945, on the Jerusalem-Bethlehem road, in the district called Talpiot, there was found a room containing ossuaries. Informed of the find, the Department of Antiquities officially appointed Doctor Eleazar Sukenik, professor of archaeology in the Hebrew university, as investigator. Following systematic excavation, he studied the question for several years (cfr. fig. 1,6.)

On October 4 of the same year, the local paper *The Palestine Post* carried sensational news. There was mention of the discovery of inscriptions which had as their subject the "lamentations of the disciples for the death of Christ." In warranting the announcement, Sukenik based his interpretation on the crosses traced on the ossuaries and on the fact that the name "Jesus," written on two of the ossuaries, was followed by the word *iou* (the beginning of the name "Jude": *Ioudah*) and by *alot* which was taken to be an exclamation of grief. The world press re-echoed the article and thus news of the find spread everywhere.

As was to be expected, scholars reacted quickly. Surprise gave way to scepticism and, subsequently, interpretations the opposite of those of Sukenik appeared. Some readers, in fact, smelt another attempt at self-advertisement. It is well known of course, that, in a conference given in Berlin on January 6, 1931, to the Archaeological Society of that city, Sukenik had produced an epitaph kept in the store-rooms of the Archaeological Museum of Jerusalem bearing the wording "Jesus, son of Joseph." Radio Berlin promptly announced that the tomb of Jesus had been found ! [9]

---

[9] *La Terra Santa* II (Febbraio, 1931), pp. 32-34 has an article with the title "A farce in three acts — The finding of the Tomb and the bones of Christ," and gives a description of the episode and of subsequent Catholic reaction. Further, in the March number, p. 54, the following was written:

It is precisely in view of what we have already seen that Sukenik was to be thought the last person in the world to give credence to an important archaeological discovery which would have demolished the commonly-held principle that it was impossible to find Christian remains in the Holy Land dating back to pre-Constantine times.

In Jerusalem, scholars felt bound to take a stand. The Director of the Department of Antiquities, R. W. Hamilton, did so by stating his views in *The Palestine Post*, October 16, 1945. He was joined by Père F.-M. Abel of the Ecole Biblique, a colleague of Vincent's. He wrote in the Egyptian daily *Rayon d'Egypte*, November 11, 1945. In general, the two scholars granted the fact that there were crosses on the ossuaries, as Sukenik had said, but they bluntly refused to discern therein any trace of Christianity. For them, the crosses drawn on the ossuaries were simply forms of the letter *taw*, and the words which Sukenik had taken for lamentations were just proper names.

Whatever the truth about the first news of the finds, it is certain that Sukenik continued to hold that the ossuaries marked with the crosses at Talpiot were Christian, not only because of their symbols but also by reason of the names they bore.

In this connection, he stated, at the first Congress of Christian Archaeology held at Syracuse in September, 1950, that "These inscriptions contain the whole dictionary of names in the New Testa-

---

"A clarification: Following our article in the last number about the inscription "Jesus, son of Joseph," Dr. Sukenik had a courteous conversation with us, in the course of which he asserted categorically that, in his Berlin conference, he had not made any mention, not even in a most indirect way, of the sensational interpretations attributed to him by the press." On the whole matter, see also L. -H. Vincent, "Epitaphe prétendue de N. S. Jésus-Christ," in *"Rendiconti della Pontificia Accademia romana di Archeologia* 7 (1931) 215-239; E. L. Sukenik, *Jüdische Grüber Jerusalem um Christi Geburt.* Jerusalem, 1931.

ment." Even the very unusual name "Sapphira" was encountered by the professor at different times on the ossuaries, sometimes written in Greek, sometimes in the original Semitic form. Amongst the titles occasionally added is the very interesting and striking term "didascalos" found by him on an ossuary found near the Hebrew University on Mount Scopus. [10]

From such statements, it is clear that Sukenik held to be Christian not only the ossuaries of Talpiot but also others discovered elsewhere. He was quite competent in this whole field and he had no interest whatever in attributing the material so found to a Christian community. However, it was the widely held opinion that all derived from some Jewish community, and the professor himself was a Jew. Therefore, we must believe him, even though he has not always gone to the trouble of providing the reasons which led to his conclusions.

His ideas were shared, or at least taken into consideration, by others. This can be argued from the *Official Guide to Israel,* published by the Department of Tourism. There we read, "About seven hundred metres behind Talpiot a tomb was excavated in 1945 and several ossuaries containing human bodies were found. Inscriptions and coins proved that the burial in the tomb took place in the years 41-42. Two ossuaries were found marked with the word "Jesus" and some others have so far been undeciphered. It has therefore been assumed that followers of Jesus had been buried in this tomb. If this assumption proves correct, this tomb would show the earliest historical evidence known about followers of Jesus." [11]

B. S. J. Isserlin wrote Sukenik's obituary. [12] He lists *inter alia,*

---

10 E. L. Sukenik, "The Earliest Records of Christianity," in *Atti del I Congresso Nazionale di Archeologia cristiana.* Rome, 1952, p. 267.

11 *Official Guide to Israel.* Tel-Aviv, 1950, p. 247.

12 B. S. J. Isserlin, "Obituary," in *Palestine Exploration Quarterly* 85 (1953) p. 79.

"the discovery of Christian epigraphical material of the earliest times." It is clear that some of those close to him were convinced about Sukenik's ideas and were not be deflected there from — and this despite many assertions to the contrary by others who, possibly, had not studied the problem as thoroughly as he himself had done.

Sukenik did not give up so easily. It seemed strange to him that the burial chambers and the ossuaries could be so devoid of Christian character. Candidly, he began to invite other Jerusalem specialists in archaeology, including Fathers Sylvester Saller and Bellarmine Bagatti, to inspect the ossuaries and discuss them with him.

Fr. Bagatti has told me how he and Fr. Saller had gone to visit the burial chamber from which the ossuaries had been removed. Then, after a three hours conversation, both Fr. Saller and himself were convinced of the sincerity of Sukenik's opinions. These were being restated once more at the time in the final edition, richly illustrated, of *The Earliest Records of Christianity*. [13]

While they did not accept Sukenik's interpretation concerning the word "Jesus," Bagatti and Saller could not but be struck by the paradox that while a Jewish scholar was trying hard to ascribe the ossuaries to Christian sources, Christian scholars, on the other hand, found it quite logical, depite arguments to the contrary, to attribute them to Jews.

Following this visit and the long conversation with Sukenik, the two Franciscan archaeologists decided to investigate the matter on their own account. Saller wrote of it in an article,[14] and Bagatti dealt with the subject in the *Rivista di Archeologia cristiana*.[15]

---

13 E. L. Sukenik, "The Earliest Records of Christianity," in *American Journal of Archaeology* 51 (1947) 351-365.

14 S. Saller, "Sepulchral Scoops," in *Around the Province* 10 (1946) 110-112.

15 B. Bagatti, "Resti cristiani in Palestina anteriori a Constantino?" in *Rivista di Archeologia cristiana* 26 (1950) 117-131.

In this he was urged on by Saller himself who often stressed the fact that Christianity did not really begin with Constantine but with Jesus Christ.

Writing of the Christian origin of the ossuaries, Saller stated, "The date, the name of Jesus and the crosses gave rise to speculations ; here you will realize that the subjective element enters. I see no objection to concluding that at least one person who was buried here was a Christian and that his name as well as that of another member of the family was Jesus (Joshua), a name very common among Jews. But to assert, as Dr. Sukenik does, that there is some direct connection between this tomb and the crucifixion of Our Lord seems to me to be going a little too far..."

Bagatti's study was fuller than Saller's. He wrote under the provocative heading (in Italian), "Christian remains in Palestine before the time of Constantine ?" He treated the discoveries at Talpiot not as something isolated but in line with other archaeological material. With his own background of scientific training in a centre of Christian archaeological study, specializing in Christian antiquities, he sought, in addition, to set the material in question within a framework which is already known from inscriptions. He noted that the Talpiot ossuaries were like those studied by Clermont-Ganneau.

Subsequently, he busied himself with the investigation of a grotto in the Shephelah at Khirbet el-Ain, opposite Judeideh, north of Jibrin, where some tombs had been changed into a columbarium. This grotto, too, was adorned with crosses.

In the same district, close by the grotto of Khirbet el-Ain, at Beit Nattif, to be precise, lamps bearing crosses and swastikas were found in a well. This discovery was made in October, 1934. As Bagatti noted, the historical background of the area was that Christians had been living there at the very time to which the archaeological material was being ascribed. Some of the inhabitants were martyred during Diocletian's persecutions. Moreover, a Chris-

Fig. 2. Khirbet el-Ain, a sepulchral grotto transformed into a columbarium (Bliss and Macalister: *Excavations in Palestine* London 1902, pl. 97)

tian community was in existence in Jerusalem itself, as is evident from the list of bishops down to 135, all of them of Jewish stock.

In explaining the symbols traced on the ossuaries and tombs, Bagatti took account of this historical and geographical background. Then, abandoning the common of Catholic scholars who had reacted against Sukenik, he pronounced them Christian.

Actually, Abel, in the article we have quoted, dealt with the controversy as to whether there was question of crosses or of *taw's*. He wrote, "We are accustomed to call it (*taw*) a *cross* because it has ended by becoming a symbol of the instrument of crucifixion. Previously, however, it had many meanings. The last letter of the

Hebrew alphabet, *taw* had this form and had no other significance than that of a *sign*. As such, it was the first letter in the word 'Torah,' that is, 'Law'."

It is clear that Abel was referring to a text of Origen's. Commenting on Ezechiel (9:4-6), the latter had written, "Jews were being questioned as to whether they had anything in the traditions of their forebears to illustrate the letter *taw*. The response was as follows. One said the letter *taw*, one of the twenty-two used by the Jews, is the last in the received order. Yet, though the last, it has been chosen to symbolize the perfection of those who, because of their virtue, bewail and mourn the sins of the people and pity the sinners. A second person said that the letter *taw* is the symbol of those who observe the Law since this, called by the Jews Torah, begins with the letter *taw*. Finally, a third, belonging to the number of those who had become Christians, said that the Old Testament writings show that the *taw* is a symbol of the cross and was a foretype of that sign which Christians are accustomed to make on their foreheads before beginning their prayers or undertaking the reading of prayers and sacred readings." [16]

From this long quotation from Origen, it is clear that the cross was held in honour and that it was reproduced not only by Christians of Gentile origin but also by Jews "who had given their names to Christ." Hence, it is not surprising that we find it on tombs.

Pondering all this, Bagatti concluded that there were not enough reasons for denying that the ossuaries under study were to be ascribed to Judaeo-Christians. This was especially so in view of the fact that, with the appearance of Christianity, Jews who remained faithful to the synagogue carefully shunned anything that would identify them with Christians, and they had a special horror of the cross.

16 Origen, *Selecta in Ezechielem; PG* 13, 799-802.

In Christian tradition, the custom of marking tombs with the cross remained constant. This is clear from the fact that ossuaries containing the relics of saints were preserved and venerated in the Church even in post-Constantine times. As already stated, one of these was found close by the wall of Jerusalem where, later on, the French Hospital of St. Louis was built.

It is only right that we should quote the concluding words of Bagatti's article for it would appear that, even at that very early stage, it expressed the wish and the hope that more findings would throw greater light on such an engrossing subject: "From what has been said, it would appear that we can conclude that, probably, here in Palestine also we have Christian material dating from pre-Constantine times. It consists of ossuaries of the first to the third century, a grotto which, at the end of the third century, was changed into a columbarium and, finally, a collection of clay lamps from the second to the third century. The reasons why we claim this material to be Christian are bound up with the common judgment on other remains in other places, with the presence of Christians in the localities where the remains were found and with consideration of the development which sacred art underwent in Palestine in the post-Constantine period. The centres of study are two: Jerusalem and the Shephelah. However, it is not unlikely that fresh research will bring more material to light in other places." [17]

The importance of the article did not escape the notice of Father Lino Randellini who drew further attention to it. He concluded, "Will new discoveries elsewhere in Palestine bring to light material similar to that examined by Fr. Bagatti? I hope so. In this case, his theory will become a reality." [18]

---

17 B. Bagatti, "Resti cristiani in Palestina anteriori a Constantino?" in *Rivista di Archeologia cristiana* 26 (1950) 131.
18 L. Randellini in *Palestra del Clero* 30 (1951) 1184.

3. *The Tombs of Sanhedria.*

In the north-west district of Jerusalem, there are to be found many burial chambers dug out of the rock. The name "Sanhedria" was given them for it was thought that they belonged to the Sanhedrin. During the last century they were only partially accessible. In 1949-1950 careful and systematic excavation was undertaken there by the Israel Department of Antiquities. The Israeli scholar, Julius Jotham-Rothschild directed the work and, at the end, gave a detailed report in two articles. [19]

For our present purpose, we should note that, one day, Jotham Rothschild observed a cross on a rock. Closer examination showed that there were three tombs marked by crosses and, in detail, the tomb given number X had three drawn on the left-hand side near the entrance leading to the central chamber. On tombs V and XIII one cross could be seen at the middle of the entrance. The archaeologist wrote, "The question which troubled me from the first day I saw the crosses is : who cut these crosses, when, and for what purpose ?" [20]

After pondering the problem he could think of one only plausible theory which would answer fully : From the earliest times, Christians who were descendants of the owners of tombs V, X and XIII and true heirs of their forebears, had been buried in the family vault. In detail, he concluded that, in tomb X, where only three *kokhim* (*loculi* : oven-shaped graves dug straight into the rock) were found, only three had contained the remains of Christians, in accord with the number of crosses found. On the other hand, in tombs numbered V and XIII, marked with one sole cross above the doorway, all the *kokhim* had been the burial places of Christians.

---

19   J. Jotham-Rothschild, "The Tombs of Sanhedriah," in *Palestine Exploration Quarterly* 84 (1952) 23-38; 86 (1954) 16-22.
20   *Idem, loc. cit.*, 1954, 18.

28

Whatever the detailed facts, the Israeli scholar found it quite understandable that Jewish converts to Christianity should be buried in the family tomb, for such was the Jewish custom. Actually, the change of religion did not annul this right. Moreover, to be deprived of the privilege of sleeping the last sleep side by side with one's own forebears was regarded as a real misfortune. [21]

4. *A sacred grotto at Bethany.*

In May, 1950, the periodical *La Terra Santa* gave news of the discovery of a grotto which had been adapted for religious worship at Bethany. As often, the find came about by chance. The Sisters of Charity, with a house near Bethany, had a grotto which they thought to alter for practical purposes. In the course of the work, it was found that the cave was marked with numerous graffiti as well as Constantine monograms (the symbol *Chi-Rho*) and crosses in the shape of a "gamma," painted and scratched on the surface.

The Sisters immediately invited professors of the Franciscan House of Biblical Studies, Jerusalem, to examine the discoveries. The material was carefully studied and, for the information of experts, a brief summary was published in the above-mentioned periodical. On this we now draw for more detail. The article is illustrated with three photos taken on March 23, and 29, 1950. At the end we read, "The many graffiti show that the grotto was frequented and venerated at various periods. Besides, the many monograms from the time of Constantine, together with "gamma" - shaped crosses, pictures and graffiti give the feeling of a Christian atmosphere. The ancient inscriptions and a study of the ceramics found on the site indicate a date in the late Roman or the Byzantine era. Finally, the locality suggests that some memory lived on especially

21 *Idem, loc. cit.,* 1954, 20.

Fig. 3. Entrance to the venerated grotto of Bethany (Mar. 22, 1950),
during the work of excavation. (From *TS* 1950, p. 148).

here in Bethany. As a possibility, we are tempted to think, for
example, of the Lord's Supper celebrated just before his Passion.
This was also sited in the grotto of Gethsemane which actually
shows some resemblances." [22]

The Sisters also invited the Dominican Fathers of the Ecole
Biblique of St. Stephen, Jerusalem, to take an interest and Frs.
Benoit and Boismard produced a most detailed study of the grotto
and the graffiti found there. [23]

Subsequently, the study of the graffiti already published by the
Dominicans was taken up by Fr. Testa. He had observed certain

---

22   Cfr. *LTS* 25 (1950) 149.
23   P. Benoit and M. E. Boismard, "Un ancien sanctuaire chrétien à Béthanie,"
in *RB* 58 (1951) 200-251.

elements which showed relationship with Jewish Christian teachings, for example, the cosmic ladder, the triangle and other designs.
There were also eschatological motifs. All of this suggested that
the grotto was venerated by Judaeo-Christians. [24] "The tenor of
these graffiti and the nature of the construction lead us to choose
from all the possible theories regarding the meaning of the monu-

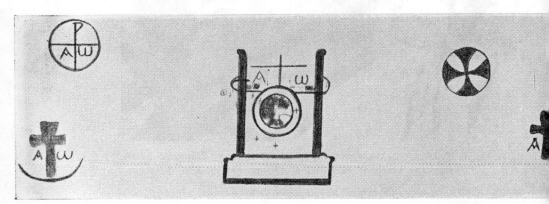

Fig. 4. Etimasia in the venerated grotto of Bethany. (From *LA*, p. 129).

ment that of the 'Lord's Supper' held in the vicinity of Bethany...
This seems to square well with what we have already put forward
relative to the Sunday Mystery of the Judaeo-Christians."

After examining some of the graffiti, Testa went on to a study
of the painted decoration. There, he discerned the throne prepared
for judgment as exemplified in the insignia of Christ and the
etimasia (theme of expectant fear) in use in the Jewish Christian
world from the fourth to the sixth century. These elements were

24   E. Testa, "Le 'Grotte dei Misteri' giudeo-cristiane," in *LA* 14 (1963-1964)
     128-131.

related to the rite of the Lord's Supper. Testa concludes : "The faithful who came to share a supper in the grotto prepared themselves to receive gifts of the Spirit promised by Christ ascended into heaven."

An examination of the material which filled the grotto yielded two coins, some fragments of glass and pieces of pottery. Unfortunately, these were overlooked in the study done by the Dominicans. They all seem to belong to the Byzantine period. This leads us to believe that, at that time, the grotto was no longer used for worship. The date coincides well with what we know about the end of the Judaeo-Christians.

From the viewpoint of palaeography, the Dominicans have established the dating of the graffiti — from the fourth to the end of the sixth or the beginning of the seventh century. One reason for the late date, according to the Dominicans, would be the slackening off of the number of pilgrims during the Arab occupation. However, it seems more consonant with the archaeological discoveries to hold that the grotto was abandoned some time before, coinciding with the gradual disappearance of the Judaeo-Christians who had worshipped there.

5. *The lamellae (metal-foil inscriptions) of Amwas, Aleppo, Beirut, Naples and Kertsch.*

At various times and places, there have been found lamellae of gold and silver. Scholars have studied them, bringing them to the attention of persons interested in the subject. Some lamellae are connected with the story of Jewish Christianity and there has been considerable progress in the study of this history. It is now certain that several lamellae express ideas which definitely belong to this current of thought. With a view to full coverage of our subject, we make mention of them here because, in a way, they are part of the history of the movement we are considering.

32

The Amwas lamella.

Towards the end of the last century, this lamella was found
in an ancient tomb of the Maccabean period at Amwas. Unfortunately, it is largely in bad shape but this has not prevented its partial decipherment. It was bought by H. Clark, United States Vice-
Consul. He kindly made it available to Fr. H. L. Vincent for a closely detailed study, and many comparisons with other similar lamellae were possible.[25] Later, it was examined by Fr. Testa.

Fig. 5. Lamella of Am-
was after P. Vincent.
(From *Revue Biblique*,
1908, p. 382).

The Amwas lamella shows Aramaic characters together with
designs, amongst which are seen a serpent and snares. There is
question of a talisman, together with an exorcism of the demon
Shamadel. It does not seem too rash a guess to suggest that this

25   L. -H. Vincent, "Amulette judéo-araméenne," in *RB* 5/17 (1908) 382-394;
     ISGC, 64-66.

lamella offers material for a comparison which could give us a still better understanding of the circumstances in which certain liturgical formulae were produced, for example, the "Commendation of the Dead" used in the Latin Rite. In this, too, there is question of the snares spread by the devil who, in the lamella, is pictured as a serpent.

It would seem that the lamella in question was not the only one discovered at Amwas. Fr. Bagatti tells me that an old resident of the place informed him that he had seen others in various tombs, placed exactly where the head of the corpse would lie. This detail harmonizes with the custom previously followed of putting a lamella in the mouth of the dead person. The idea behind this was that the soul came forth by way of the mouth and that it was in need of help for the difficult climb up the cosmic ladder. [26]

The Aleppo lamella.

This was found at the beginning of the present century and was bought by Fr. Giacinto Tonizza, O. F. M. while resident in Aleppo (1899-1905). It is kept in the museum of the Franciscan House of Biblical Studies of "The Flagellation." There it was sent by Tonizza himself, an assiduous collector of antiquities. [27] The lamella carries the inscription, "found near the river Euphrates" which is based on information given by Tonizza (cfr. fig. 6). In 1906 it was studied by M. Schwab who produced a description, transcription and photos of it. [28]

---

26   E. Testa, *ISGC*, 64-66.

27   P. Castellana, "Un illustre numismatico francescano," in *LTS* 22 (1947) 172-178.

28   M. Schwab, "Une amulette judéo-araméenne," in *Journal Asiatique*, Janv.-Févr. 1906, 5-15.

קמיע טב לתום לו פתגמא חד
קדושא בר בון ובקר ישיאשמן גבי
דמיאל מנאר יה עדו אהיהא
אחמה אהוה אחמה וחשדו ה
אלהיהוא את מאצו כרע
טלמי ולמאבמענא כל נדך ה
דן יהוה אהיה יהודאל שדי אש
אל ב ישׁחו בַּ חוק אהית ומ
מלך ין מענה יֹם אשׁ מקעבו ח
אלצ רעשהן חרן סד וחד חבמה
וחביחו יה רֹ ה ו עדולוד ודר
חיָא שם לעלם ועד דרום ופעם
ושמאול ומעוב לאחו בנֹגפוֹה
חארץ ויעצ ו רשׁעם מעמה ק
תנער חטלנית ורוח וכר ונקבה
מן אפֿמן נהתה באמרבן מעאים
ואדבעים ושׁמתה אבריה ומאדבע
מאותעם קרבין ובל תשׁית לב נכל
עליה בפוה תיחל מן זולתו בצל
חמה כמו עפו לבנה וכמעלותיה א
נַאבּגֿעֿבֿאֿכֿאֿמֿבֿ יה קֿשׁוֹה
מֿאֿבֿאֿ יׄהֿ ۽ כֿוׄۥۥ؛ۻۻۦۻ פٍۥۥۻۻۛۛ
אמֿן אמן סלה ۾ חללויה

אלהו מערות ובשם אוגרית מן
מראות יפא ובמלכות אבלנה
אלברה נאתה לבאת קטבו יֹ
מראות חדן

(Fig. 6. Lamella of Aleppo — star/sun symbols drawing)

משביע אני עליכם הפגעוֹחק
והאש והעריח בי ץ מים לי
בי ן משבת לשבת בי מֹשֹחֹ
לשעד בין עהדש אלדר שׁ משֹנֹ
אני עליכם בשם ימיֹן ומׄ
תוקפוביה יה היהוה בו
עבאות אלהו ישראל
לחוי חקי

It contains inscriptions in Aramaic together with designs which, as happens very rarely, are explained by the text itself. Fr. Ronzevalle who interviewed Schwab declares that the lamella "if I am not mistaken, offers a subject of interest equal to, if not surpassing, that of all other magical texts published." Vincent stated that, though many doubtful objects are described as originating in Aleppo, in this instance there is nothing unusual in the matter and it can be accepted without further qualification. [29]

It is to be noted that this lamella also belonged to a tomb. Hence, as in the case of the one just discussed, it can be viewed as a kind of "laissez-passer" in favour of the dead person. He had to leave the grave to undertake the journey to the throne of God. [30]

The Beirut lamellae.

Here there is question of two lamellae originating in Beirut and both pertinent to our subject. The first, in Greek, was sent to the Museum of the Louvre in March, 1900. Information accompanying it stated that it was found in a tomb in Beirut. It was studied by A. Heron de Villefosse. [31] He took it for a magical tablet. The examination resulted in transcription and a partial translation, though no illustration is provided. The lamella is composed of 120 lines, quite small and written to protect one Alexandra against the devil. It ends with an exorcism. It reminds us of various symbolic details found in connection with the cosmic ladder, amongst them the seven stars and the angels who guard them. [32]

---

29 L. -H. Vincent, "Amulette judéo-araméenne, in *RB* 5/17 (1908) 392.

30 E. Testa, *ISGC*, 52-59.

31 A. Héron de Villefosse, "Tablette magique de Beyrouth conservée au Musée du Louvre," in *Florilegium Melchior de Vogüé*. Paris, 1909, 287-295.

32 B. Bagatti, *LEC*, 232.

The other lamella, purchased in Beirut in 1925 by Charles Virolleaud, is in Aramaic. The buyer took the trouble to show it to several scholars. Arthur Cowley of Oxford expressed a wish to study it and it was sent off to him. Unfortunately, it never arrived. So, scholars had to be content with basing their studies of it on two fairly good photos taken when it was bought. The orientalist, Dupont-Sommer, made a copy from the photos and, in a book devoted entirely to this lamella, states, "In any case, one can say that, overall, while the two pictures published herein do not agree perfectly with the lost original, they have preserved the essentials. We hope that, one day with luck, the famous document so unfortunately lost will be restored to us." [33]

This lamella has twenty-one lines and is illustrated by designs. Amongst them is the eight-pointed star, the well-known symbol of the angels. Testa [34] holds that the teaching expressed in it does not vary from that in vogue in the primitive Jerusalem Church. Besides, Dupont-Sommer himself had already written in this regard, "Our lamella in Aramaic is, as we shall see, of Christian origin. In this sense it is, up till the present, something unique." [35] Today, when studies on the early Jerusalem Church are more advanced, we cannot quite call this document "unique." Nevertheless, it still forms one of the choice items surviving from Jewish Christianity.

The Naples lamella.

Besides lamellae bearing inscriptions of a funerary character, we have others with pictures. Some of these are connected with the history of Jewish Christianity. One of the best known of this

---

33   A. Dupont-Sommer, *La doctrine gnostique de la lettre "waw" d'après une lamelle araméenne inédite.* Paris, 1946, 8.
34   E. Testa, *ISGC*, 59-64.
35   A. Dupont-Sommer, *op. cit.*, 8.

type is that kept in the National Museum in Naples. It was published by the Italian archaeologist, Carlo Cecchelli. [36] In form, it is rather primitive and shows the cross surmounted by Christ, with two angels in prayer. It carries some wording in Greek. This subject resembles that found on medals discovered in Palestine and Syria and recalls the "personified cross" one of the symbolic ways of expressing the mystery of the Redemption according to Jewish Christian thought. [37]

There are three other lamellae of the same kind which are less well known but still of interest. One of these was found at Kertsch in the Crimea and edited by Bamm. [38] It is of primitive workmanship and shows the cross standing on a pedestal adorned with seven

Fig. 7.   Lamella   of Crimea
(From Bamm, p. 172)

36   C. Cecchelli, *Il trionfo della croce. La croce e i santi segni prima e dopo Costantino*. Roma, 1954, 170.
37   B. Bagatti, *LEC*, 181-184.
38   P. Bamm, *Welten des Glaubens*. München, 1959, 172.

points. The cross is surmounted by the head of Christ and is surrounded by four X's and smaller dots.

6. *Two letters on papyrus, and a parchment booklet.*

The letter of Bar Kokhba.

In 1952, at Murabba'at, there was found an ancient document
written on papyrus. The find caused much excitement amongst scholars who proceeded to transcribe and interpret it in various ways.
J. T. Milik was the first to publish it. [39] According to his translation,
Simeon Bar Kokhba, after his greeting, made reference to Yeshu'a
Ben Ghilgola and then stated: "I take heaven to witness against
me. If you do not break with the Galileans whom you have been
helping, I will put irons on your feet, as I have already done with
Ben 'Aphlul." It is clear that the letter derives from the time when
the Jews, led by Bar Kokhba (or Koseba), were waging war against
Hadrian.

Milik adds a commentary and interpretation to his literal translation. According to him, [40] the Galileans mentioned in the letter
are not combatants but Christians of Jewish origin. "It probably
follows that these 'Galileans,' not being combatants (according to
the strict topographical meaning and lacking any hint of reference
to a Jewish sect in Galilee) can only be Christians or, more exactly,
Judaeo-Christians. That Bar Kokhba persecuted such people is clear
from Justin Martyr [41] and Eusebius." [42]

Milik stresses the importance of the document regarding the
evidence it might provide relative to the situation of Christians

39   J. T. Milik, "Une lettre de Siméon Bar Kokheba," in *RB* 60 (1953) 276-294.
40   *Idem, art. cit.,* 287.
41   *Apol.* I, 31 (*PG* 6, 376).
42   *Chron. ad ann. Abr.* 2149 (according to the Armenian version.)

Fig 8. Letter of Bar Cokhba
(From *Les Grottes de Mu-*
rabba'ât II, tav. 46).

during the Second Revolt and of their existence in Palestine.
"Granted, this evidence has reference only to details which remain
problematical. But, added to the witness of Justin and Eusebius,
it neverthless represents the oldest archaeological document dealing
with the presence of Christians in Palestine. though the other documents present even more problems than this letter. On the one
hand, Simeon Bar Kokhba's reactions to the Christians and, on the
other, the sympathy of the two "poputtchiks", Ben 'Aphlul and
Yeshu'a Ben Ghilgola (stated so vividly in the sparse lines of this
short note) are eloquent and priceless for historians of the first
centuries of our era and are precious in the memory of every
Christian." [43]

Inevitably, other scholars became interested in the document
because of its reference either to the Second Jewish War or to primitive Christianity. Amongst others, Yigael Yadin [44] translates it
thus : "I take heaven to witness against me : mobilize from the
Galileans whom I have saved (or whom you have saved) everyone;
for (otherwise) I shall put iron on your feet as I did to Ben 'Aphlul."

43   J. T. Milik. *art. cit.*, 294.
44   Y. Yadin, *The Message of the Scrolls*. New York, 1957, 71-72.

The noted Israeli scholar queries whether the Galileans mentioned in the letter are Christians (as others like Milik interpret them to be) or whether they are simply members of some sect in Galilee who lived in the vicinity of Khirbet Qumran itself. As Yadin does not wish to commit himself, he adds laconically, "We cannot give a final answer." Thus, he fails to agree either with the translation or with Milik's interpretation of the ancient find.

Various other readings of the document are proposed by scholars — evidence of the difficulty in deciphering such inscriptions. [45] Regarding the title "Galileans," we may note that M. Delcor [46] has stated that such a title was not given Christians until later, that is, in the fourth century under Julian the Apostate. In the second century, precisely in the period of the letter under discussion, it was used to designate individuals belonging to an anonymous sect. In fact, it is in this sense that it is used by Justin [47] and Hegesyppus. [48]

In the final edition of his work, [49] Milik himself alters his original interpretation by stating that the letter contains a threat of imprisonment against the leader who continues to harm the Galileans. Milik takes it that these latter are civil refugees with homes in Galilee but now living in towns in southern Judah. Milik grants that his original theory, according to which there is question of Judaeo-Christians, is not less satisfactory. This remains the opinion of more recent students of the problem.

---

45   E. Testa, "Hgll'ym — "Nome dispregiativo dei Giudeo-cristiani," in *Euntes Docete* 10 (1957) 281-284.

46   M. Delcor, "Murabba'ât," in *Dictionnaire de la Bible* — Suppl. 5. coll. 1393-1394.

47   Dialogue 80, 4 (*PG* 6, 665).

48   *Ecclesiastical History* iv, xxii, 7 (PG 20, 381).

49   J. T. Milik, *Les grottes de Murabba'ât. Discoveries in the Judean Desert* II. Oxford, 1961, 159-161.

Letter of Gabriel, "Sinner."

Another papyrus letter written by one Gabriel, "Sinner" was found in 1953 by a Belgian archaeological mission digging at Khirbet el-Mird, that is, in the ruins of ancient Hircania which was changed by St. Sabas into the monastery of Castellion. Milik studied this document also, giving the first transcription and the corresponding translation and interpretation.[50]

As in the case of the Letter of Bar Kokhba, he felt bound to revise his first opinion [51]. He published a second transcription and translation somewhat different from that originally presented.

The letter is in Aramaic. Milik first dated it in the seventh century, then in the eighth to the tenth century. The document was sent by a certain Gabriel, "Sinner" to the superior of the laura "of our holy father" (or, possibly, "of our lords and our fathers"). The sender begs prayers "because of the tribe, on account of whom my hearts trembles" (first edition) or "by reason of the disturbance because of which my heart is broken" (revised edition).

Depending on the reading accepted, this short document is of greater or less importance for the history of monasticism in Palestine. The first translation by Milik would suggest some outside source of trouble which upset the whole community of monks living at Castellion. There could be question of a nomad tribe disturbing the area by raids and causing widespread panic. On the other hand, the second interpretation would imply some quite personal trouble in Gabriel himself, perhaps some internal malaise. This has only a very relative value for history.

We cannot determine whether the letter was written at Castellion and then, for some unknown reason, left undespatched. Per-

---

50   J. T. Milik, "Une inscription et une lettre en araméen christo-palestinien," in *RB* 60 (1953), 533-539.
51   J. T. Milik, "The Monastery of Kastellion," in *Biblica* 42 (1961), 25-26.

haps, it was sent from an unknown locality to the monastery of St. Sabas and duly received. Later, it ended up at Castellion where it was rediscovered. It is precisely for these reasons that Milik's deductions both as to the circumstances and the date of writing remain theoretical.

This brief note, valuable in the history of monasticism in Palestine, also provides evidence of the use of the ancient Aramaic language. It can be connected with the symbols, inscriptions and other archaeological documents to form a link in the chain which proves that Aramaic was used in Palestine, that it was the language of the Judaeo-Christians and that it lived on amongst the people and clergy in various places in Palestine and Transjordan until the times of the High Middle Ages.

A booklet in Aramaic.

Connected with the letter of Gabriel, "Sinner" is a booklet written on parchment in the same Aramaic tongue. It was found, also, in the Kidron river bed. During the Belgian excavations of 1935, it was given by the head workman to Canon R. De Langhe and is now kept in Louvain. M. Baillet [52] has provided a good description of it together with a partial translation. The nature of the letter itself, having some affinity with magical formulae, makes it difficult to decipher fully. Its Christian character is apparent from the cross with two horns, prayers against scorpions and vipers and the main prayer contained therein: "You who have been crucified, have mercy on us!" The booklet also has recipes for the making of inks.

Baillet writes, "Study of the handwriting should help us fix the date. But, what problems we meet with in the palaeography

---

52 M. Baillet, "Un livret magique en christo-palestinien à l'Université de Louvain," in *Le Muséon* 76 (1963), 375-401.

of Christian Palestine!" Thus, as a result of comparison with the letter of Khirbet el-Mird, he tentatively suggests the sixth century. The last named letter was the only other one known at the time.

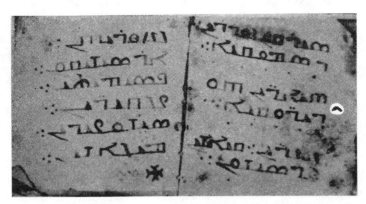

Fig. 9. Two pages of the Aramaic booklet found near the Kedron (From *Le Muséon*, 1963, tav. III).

So, this document also reminds us that we are still a long way from fixing a certain date for many writings of this kind. For this reason, we are not able to say whether they represent a "continuity" or a "renaissance" of the ancient culture founded on Judaism. Yet, they do show that amongst the monks of Palestine there were some who had been brought up on Jewish Christian culture. This is confirmed by literary sources which attest that such persons lived in Syria. An example is St. Jerome's famous master in the monastery of Chalcis. Also, there were people as late as the fifth century who wished to keep up the custom of reburial in ossuaries.[53]

---

53 B. Bagatti, *LEC*, 69 and 220; E. Testa, "L'uso degli Ossuari tra i monaci di Siria," in *LTS* 39 (1963), 36-41.

7. Stone inscriptions from Syria and Transjordan.

In the last century, already, inscriptions found in Syria on tombstones and door-lintels had attracted notice of scholars. Well known are the collections made by Rev. W. Ewing (edited in the *Palestine Exploration Fund Quarterly Statement*, 1895), that illustrated in the volumes by Prentice (New York, 1908), that of the University of Princeton's expedition (Leiden, 1921), that of the Jesuit Fathers at Beirut and that of Tchalenko (Paris, 1953-1958).

Some of these inscriptions have intrigued the experts by reason of their special character. One of the Tafas inscriptions states, "James and Samuel and Clematios, their father, built this synagogue." Alt[54] took into account the place of discovery and other inscriptions found nearby and concluded that there is question of a synagogue for the use of Judaeo-Christians. Another reason is that Tafas is not far from Kokaba, a centre of the Ebionites. Regarding these, St. Epiphanius[55] tells us that they called their places of assembly not "churches" but "synagogues." Besides, there was found in the same district an inscription which speaks of a synagogue used by a community of Marcionites.

Subsequently, with more finds relative to the Judaeo-Christians, it has been possible to establish more in detail that many of the inscriptions found in Syria are to be traced to currents of thought common in the Church of the Circumcision. This is true, not only with regard to the shape of the crosses, symbols, sacred letters and other details, but also with reference to the concepts of angels. From the comparisons we may take it that if not actually made up of Christians deriving from Judaism itself, the Christian communities of those places were influenced by Jewish Christian teaching.

54   J. -B. Frey, *Corpus Inscriptionum Iudaicarum*, I, n. 861
55   *PG* 41, 436.

The district of Kerak in Transjordan, too, shows Jewish Christian influence. It seems more homogeneous than that observed in the material found in Syria. This close relationship is to be attributed, no doubt, to the smallness of the area. There it was possible for Christian communities to have closer contracts with one another.

A great mass of inscriptions, which had remained unedited for centuries, has been collected and published by Reginetta Canova. [56] The material was brought together during the years 1936-1940 and it was subsequently studied and edited.

The inscriptions are almost all of a funerary character dating from the fourth to the eighth century. The most characteristic feature is that of the number-letters inserted into the text itself. This seems a little disconcerting but, in reality it represents a deep theological meaning known only to those who were acquainted with a like way of expressing religious ideas about the dead.

Mrs. Canova also had the good fortune to come across a small cemetery with steles still in position. It was characterized by various types of crosses, some of which undoubtedly bear Jewish Christian details. Thus, her study represents a valuable contribution to our knowledge of the history of Jewish Christianity.

56   R. Canova, *Iscrizioni e monumenti protocristiani nel paese di Moab.* Città del Vaticano, 1954.

Chapter II

THE NEW DISCOVERIES

When Clermont-Ganneau stated that some of the ossuaries found at Bat'n el-Hawa belonged to Judaeo-Christians, his opinion was not very warmly received by the archaeologists. Yet, it was not entirely ignored. As we have seen in the preceding chapter, some scholars busied themselves with the same line of research and had the good fortune to find other, similar material in different places.

Thanks to deeper study, which set the material in its proper historical and geographical background, and made possible comparison with other finds, the theories of Clermont-Ganneau gained more and more followers, especially amongst Jewish and Protestant experts. Catholic specialists, on the other hand, with the exception of the Franciscan archaeologists, steered clear of them, being certain of the commonly held principle that Christian communities just did not exist in Palestine prior to the period of Constantine.

Scholars, including those already convinced of the presence of Jewish Christianity in the Holy Land before that time, earnestly hoped that more material would be found to throw further light on the subject. This finally came about and in such abundance that the years 1953-1963 can be called "the golden age" so far as Jewish Christian finds are concerned.

1. *The Jewish Christian Burial Ground of "Dominus Flevit."*

The excavations.

On the western slope of the Mount of Olives, there is a small property called "Dominus Flevit" ("The Lord Wept") where, at the end of the last century, the Franciscan Custody of the Holy Land built a small shine commemorating Jesus' lamentation over the Holy City. More recently, the Custody purchased a plot of ground to the south, lying between the two paths, the middle and the southern, which climb Olivet from Gethsemane. A wall had to be built to protect it. In April, 1953, diggings for the foundations of this latter began. Unexpectedly, the workmen came across the remains of a cemetery which had remained quite unknown. It was found that the burial ground had been in use from the first to the fourth century A. D.

In the cemetery, two periods are clearly discernible: the first extending almost to the end of the second Jewish War in 135 and marked by tombs in the shape of *kokhim*. The later period was characterized by graves in the form of *arcosolia* (trough-shaped graves dug parallel with the walls).

Fr. Bagatti was commissioned by the Custody to take charge of the excavations which followed and to prepare reports on them. In a room, not far from the path to the south of the Franciscan property which leads upwards from Gethsemane to the top of Mt. Olivet, he found fourteen ossuaries quite similar to those discovered by Clermont-Ganneau not far from "Dominus Flevit," and also resembling others found by Sukenik on the Jerusalem-Bethlehem highway.

On one he saw a cross. In another he found traces of a "Constantine monogram." Further, he noted names with a New Testament ring, for example, Jairus, Martha, Maria, Simon Bar Jonah, and so on. There came to light also the proper name of a woman,

48

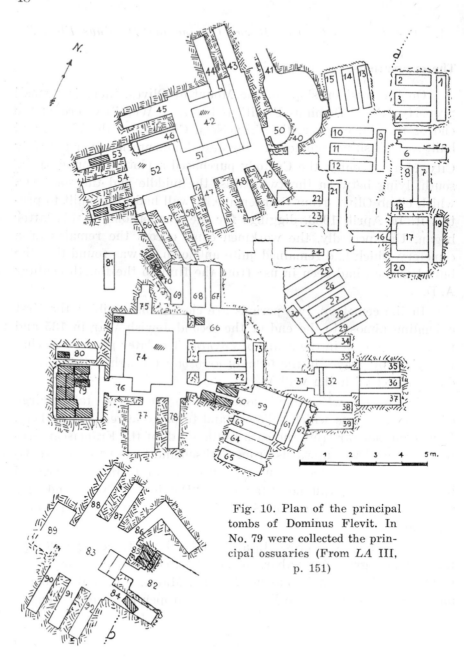

Fig. 10. Plan of the principal tombs of Dominus Flevit. In No. 79 were collected the principal ossuaries (From *LA* III, p. 151)

Fig. 11. The room 79 with the principal ossuaries(From *LA* III, p. 161)

"Šalamzion" ("Greetings to Zion") which had already been observed in the discoveries by Clermont-Ganneau at Bat'n el-Hawa. One
of the tombs at "Dominus Flevit" had been countersigned with a *X*
(*Chi*), chiselled into the stone by the same hand as had fashioned
the name of the deceased. Moreover, it was engraved by the same
deep-pointed instrument as had formed the characters of the inscription itself. The ossuaries showed evidence of like markings .

Once again, the problem arose : to whom did these tombs belong?
Were they Jewish or Jewish Christian? Bagatti studied the "Con-
stantine monogram" in all its different shapes and purposes, especial-
ly as adapted to funerary monuments. He decided that it was
Christian. No other explanation or interpretation seemed tenable.
According to Bagatti, the cross, used precisely on ossuaries, was

50

Fig. 12. View of the principal tombs (From *LA* III, p. 154).

to be understood as a *taw* but conceived in a new light, that of Judaeo-Christians. The tomb must have belonged to people of this tradition. This was supported by the evidence of the proper names inscribed, as also by comparisons with previous finds.

Interpretation of the discoveries.

For the benefit of scholars, Bagatti published a preliminary
report on the first, main results.[1] Interest in the finds and their
interpretation was immediate. Monsignor Salvatore Garofalo gave
them prominent notice in an article in *L'Osservatore Romano*.
Noting that the diggings were not yet ended, and that there was
question still of early results, he added: "Up till the present, however, there is enough material at hand to attract the attention
of the experts and even the intelligent curiosity of the public."

"It is our intention simply to report the discoveries, without
pretending to repeat what has already been done or to put forward
any personal appraisal, especially as the subject is quite delicate
and complex.... These are the data provided by the finely-documented
study by Fr. Bagatti, enriched by quite appropriate illustrations,
maps and sketches. It brings new material to the 'dossier' relative
to the custom of using the sign of the cross and the Christian monogram during the first centuries. This is a subject which has interested scholars deeply in recent years."[2]

In *Revue Biblique*,[3] the Dominican Fathers brought readers
up to date with a description of the burial chamber and the ossuaries. It was stated, "Besides this, there are symbols which Fr.
Bagatti, after deep, scientific discussion, suggests are recognizable
as Christian..... Having dealt with the various explanations hitherto
proposed relative to other archaeological finds, Fr. Bagatti concludes
that here, once again, a Christian meaning is probably involved.

1   B. Bagatti, "Scoperta di un cimitero giudeo-cristiano al 'Dominus Flevit',"
     in *LA* 3 (1952-1953), 149-184.

2   S. Garofalo, "Scoperta d'un cimitero giudeo-cristiano del I secolo sul Monte
     degli Ulivi," in *L'Osservatore Romano*, Dicembre 25, 1953.

3   P. Benoit in *RB* 61 (1954) 568-570.

52

Fig. 13. Inscription of Salamzion with an X which marks the name. (From *LA* III, p. 167)

Fig. 14. Inscription of Martha and Mary (From *LA* III, p. 158)

Fig. 15. Inscription of Simeon Bar Jonah (From *LA* III p. 162).

He stresses the point that these latest discoveries actually throw light on the former which were imperfectly explained, also that they build up to a firm indication that one should not reject *a priori* divergencies from the current ideas on the antiquity of the Christian symbols. Certainly, a Christian community was in existence in Jerusalem in the first century. Therefore, there is nothing strange in the fact that tombs of these people should be found. It is quite natural that those first brethren should have manifested their new faith by means of some symbol distinguishing them from other Jews.... If the prudent and well-documented interpretation turns out to be true, no one can ignore the importance of this find."

We think that Benoit was the author of another note in *Revue Biblique*. In it he returns to the same subject and presents a report to the Fifth Congress of Archaeology held in Aix-en-Provence in September, 1954.[4] Having spoken of the discovery at "Dominus Flevit" and the opinions expressed about it, he concludes : "It would therefore seem necessary to revise ideas hitherto held on the antiquity of these Christian symbols."

Basing his statements on the news and assessment found in *Revue Biblique,* the archaeologist, A. Parrot, found it natural that the discovery and its interpretation should stand as evidence of the presence of a primitive Christian community. He writes : "The mass of documents can hardly be given any other interpretation. Of great importance in every respect are these proofs which throw light on the presence of a Christian community at Jerusalem. The tradition in *Acts* had already spoken of its rapid spread from Pentecost Day onwards."[5]

---

4   P. Benoit, "Les découvertes paléochrétiennes en Palestine arabe entre 1939 et 1954," in *Actes du Ve Congrès international d'Archéologie chrétienne.* Città del Vaticano — Paris, 1955, 23-37.

5   A. Parrot, *Golgotha et Saint-Sépulcre.* Paris, 1955, 92-93.

54

Both Parrot and Benoit were well conversant with the surroundings of Jerusalem and the material of the first centuries
which had been brought to light. It is clear that, having taken New
Testament data into consideration, they found no difficulty in ad-
mitting that there is question of archaeological remains of the primitive Christian community in Jerusalem.

Other Bible specialists, starting with the archaeological results
in question, have endeavoured to connect them with passages in the
Scriptures. Thus, in his Commentary on Ezechiel, H. G. May writes:
"The early Christians naturally interpreted this mark as the sign
of the cross and an anticipation of the crucifixion. The cross or *taw*
is found on first-century A.D. ossuaries." [6] It is clear that, in this
comment, May based his words on the discoveries on Mt. Olivet
and at Talpiot.

However, if a Bible specialist can appreciate the reasons why
archaeologists hold firmly that the material in question belongs to
Judaeo-Christians (precisely because it reflects a Jewish mentality),
it is not so easy for people who live outside Palestine and have at
hand only and always such material as derives from the Gentile-
Christian stream of culture.

So, it is not surprising to read in *Rivista di Archeologia cristiana* a brief résumé of Bagatti's work and to find the following
(ascribed to A. Ferrua): "Bagatti thinks that they are Christian
tombs and symbols because it is only through reference to Christian
teaching that they can be explained. Mons. Garofalo in *L'Osservatore
Romano*, December 25, p. 3, agrees with him. Also in agreement
will be Sukenik who, in substance, follows the same reasoning as
Bagatti. But, instead of arguing on the grounds of some cryptic
symbols for the presence of Christianity in a cemetery, it would

6   H. G. May, *The Interpreter's Bible*, VI. New York, 1956, 112-113.

be better first to fix the religious nature of the tomb and thence to deduce the value of the cryptography." [7]

While writing his book *Il trionfo della Croce*,[8] C. Cecchelli came across Bagatti's article "Resti cristiani in Palestina anteriori a Constantino?" He noted that the author of the article admitted the Christian character of the ossuaries as "possible and not as certain." He then expressed the hope that other proofs would be forthcoming. In the meantime, he also accepted the interpretation as a possibility.

When the preliminary report on the diggings at "Dominus Flevit" appeared in *Liber Annuus*, Cecchelli felt it needful to add an appendix to his book in which he spoke of "most recent discoveries of Christian symbols in Palestine." He went on: "the new finds are taking on a special importance" and noted that the marks seen on the ossuaries were discovered anew in the burial chambers. They were symbols of identification, and also of Christian salvation. He states, moreover, that "the period followed the practices of the Jewish religion, adding thereto acts of worship of Christ. There is nothing surprising in the fact that their tombs have been found in a large Jewish cemetery." He goes on: "Bagatti queries (always with great caution) whether the Christians of St. James the Less' time could have had the idea of the saving power of the Cross, like St. Paul." He then quotes the words, "It is by no means proven that the Jerusalem Christians did not recognize the value of Christ's death and that they rejected the Cross." He then states: "In recent times, archaeology is seriously contradicting those worthy, but tendentious scholars, who had been evaporating as myth the traditions of the Church."

---

7   A. Ferrua, in *Rivista di Archeologia cristiana* 30 (1954), 268.
8   C. Cecchelli, *Il trionfo della croce. La croce e i santi segni prima e dopo Costantino.* Rome, 1954, 63, 161-165.

The definitive publication of results.

When the excavation of the cemetery came to an end, Bagatti collaborated with J. T. Milik and described the results in a book in which all the inscriptions were studied anew.[9] The preliminary article in *Liber Annuus* had given only hints. The book itself gave full information on the abundance of the material discovered. Chapter VI, for example, is a deep study of the subject, "investigations on the condition of the dead" set against the primitive background. It concludes: "Every so often around Jerusalem, we find Jewish names written without further explanation and dating from 33 to 135. It is not right to say simply that they are 'Jewish.' The terms 'of Jewish origin' should be used, for they belong to *believers in Christ*. But, is there nothing to indicate a distinction between the different religions? Some Palestinian archaeologists, going by local excavations, have come to the conclusion that they can differentiate details such as names and symbols and so arrive at this distinction. Their familiarity with ordinary Jewish data has led them to distinguish other material which is not relative thereto. This latter is attributed to the Judaeo-Christians."

As is clear, Bagatti goes his own way, continually presenting new material and arguments to prove the presence of a Jewish Christian Church early in Palestine. He does not share Ferrua's belief that criteria such as were used in Rome can be applied likewise in Jerusalem. The observations of Jotham-Rothschild on family graves have to be borne in mind here.

Agreement and dissent.

In general, Bagatti's conclusions on the burial ground found at "Dominus Flevit" were warmly welcomed by scholars. For ex-

9   B. Bagatti and J. T. Milik, *GSDF*.

ample, R. Motte [10] says that "Some ossuaries undoubtedly bear Christian symbols." R. North [11] follows the same line of thought. J. Van der Ploeg [12] noted the restrained language used by Bagatti and concluded that the archaeological remains as found, described and interpreted are of great interest, for they belong to the oldest Christian community in Jerusalem, made up of faithful who came from families who were still Jewish.

P. Testini [13] accepts the theory that the ossuaries found at "Dominus Flevit" belong to Christians. In this regard he writes: "Subsequent on discoveries of an impressive series of monuments (explained by biblical and patristic references), Fr. Bagatti has recently shown that before 135 the Jewish Christian community in Palestine was using the letter *taw* on tombs, thus making reference to the Cross and representing a symbol of salvation in accord with the well-known passage in Ezechiel (9:4). The use of the sign may have developed because of the need to make a distinction between themselves and Jewish confreres who, in turn, had for the same reason adopted the use of the symbol of the candelabrum." Testini stresses the fact that the finds "open up new perspectives on the discussion of the problem of the existence of the cross as an early symbol of Christian life in the first centuries down to its triumphal appearance under Constantine." [14]

In Germany, Philip Seidensticker spread the news of the archaeological finds at "Dominus Flevit." He was able to see the first finds personally during his stay in Jerusalem (1953-1954). Subsequently, when the material was removed to the Museum of the

---

10 R. Motte, "Ossuaires," in *Dictionnaire de la Bible — Suppl.* 6, coll. 945-946.
11 R. North, "Ossuarium," in *Lexicon für Theologie und Kirche*, 7, 1962, coll. 1270-1271.
12 J. Van Der Ploeg, in *Journal of Semitic Studies* 5 (1960), 81-82.
13 P. Testini, *Archeologia cristiana.* Rome, 1958, 295-298.
14 *Idem, op. cit.*, 298.

House of Biblical Studies at "The Flagellation," he was able to view it and study it at ease. He makes mention of it in the book of memoirs of his stay in Palestine.[15] Later, he dealt with the matter in three scientific articles.[16]

Reviewing the book published on the finds at "Dominus Flevit," Francesco Vattioni writes: "One can argue about, or disagree on the subject of the religion of the dead. Nevertheless, one must grant the soberness of the presentation which is highly documented."[17] This qualified assessment can be explained and understood if we take account of the review which Fr. Roland de Vaux had published in the meantime in *Revue Biblique*.[18]

Dealing with the "Constantine monogram" de Vaux wrote: "I do not know what import it has for the ossuary of 'Dominus Flevit,' but nothing shows that it may have been a Christian symbol."[19] De Vaux made similar decisions regarding other symbols described and interpreted by Bagatti. In a word, so far as de Vaux was concerned, the Christian character of the burial ground of "Dominus Flevit" was not quite proven.

This markedly negative assessment did not derive from a study of the material itself since de Vaux produced nothing to support his claim that the arguments put forward by Bagatti did not hold. It would seem that he took his stand simply on his own authority. Nevertheless, it could not but affect people who had no opportunity of studying the finds at "Dominus Flevit" personally.

Thus, for example, James B. Pritchard dealt with the question of the Christian character of the ossuaries which had been found.

---

15   Ph. Seidensticker, *Ins heilige Land. Werl*, 1955, 166.
16   In *Bibel und Kirche* 14 (1959), 13-19; in *Franziskanische Studien* 40 (1958), in *Echo der Zeit*, March 1, 1959, 16.
17   F. Vattioni, in *Rivista Biblica* 7 (1959), 81-83.
18   R. De Vaux, in *RB* 66 (1959), 299-301.
19   *Idem, art. cit.*, 300.

He wrote: "The appearance of the so-called Constantine monogram, X with a superimposed P when taken with proper names, which correspond to those found in the New Testament, has led the excavator to consider the burials in tomb 79 as Christian. This conclusion has been disputed with considerable force by R. de Vaux in *Revue Biblique* (66 (1959) 299-301). This volume is an extremely lucid presentation of important material." [20]

Another negative decision was that of M. Avi-Yonah. He thought that the Christian character of the ossuaries of "Dominus Flevit" remained unproven. [21] Reviewing Bagatti's book, he raised two objections against the author's conclusions, though he did not provide any relevant documentation. He stated that immediately one postulates a Jewish element, there is the possibility that there were other Jewish sects who could have used the sign *taw* on tombs; second, account must be made of the very small number of Christians then in existence in Palestine.

In this connection, Bagatti and Testa undertook further research to see whether the first objection could be sustained on the basis of any particular text. They found no evidence that other sects might have used the *taw* sign on tombs even in Christian times. On the contrary, it was proven that Jews had a horror of doing anything of the kind. Regarding the second point, that of the allegedly small number of Christians, it is clear that Avi-Yonah did not take account of what Christian sources of the time have to offer. *Acts,* for example, in 2:41; 4:4; 21:20 speaks of thousands of converts to Christianity. Hegesyppus, quoted by Eusebius, [22] states that many notables embraced the Christian faith, so much so that the Scribes and Pharisees grew alarmed, fearful that the whole nation would be converted to Christ.

---

20   J. B. Pritchard, in *American Journal of Archaeology* 64 (1960), 302.
21   M. Avi-Yonah, in *Israel Exploration Journal* 11 (1961), 91-94.
22   *Ecclesiastical History* II, xxiii, 10 (*PG* 20, 200).

Discounting Christian sources is a tendency to be seen likewise in Thérèse Frankfort's review of Bagatti's book. She says: "Besides, the existence of a Christian community in Palestine in the first century is problematical. Though evidenced in the Christian sources, it is not mentioned in Jewish texts nor by pagan writers, even when these latter refer to Christians in other parts of the Roman Empire." [23] Otherwise, the writer speaks highly of the book and ends by stating that it is "primordial" so far as the inscriptions and illustrations are concerned. This holds also with respect to continual reference to other finds and the lists of pottery and glassware. All this provides closer detail for further precision in this field of study.

The writer's refusal to admit the existence of a primitive Christian community in Jerusalem on the grounds that information about it lies only in Christian sources appears quite strange. One would rather have expected such a decision on the part of non-Christian authors.

A romantic element enters.

Before ending these short summaries, we cannot pass over an amusing episode to which the discoveries in question happened to give rise. Amongst the inscriptions found on the ossuaries of "Dominus Flevit," there was one in Hebrew which read *Šime'on bar Jonah*. Scholars agree that this name is to be ascribed to some namesake of St. Peter and nothing more. Bagatti thinks there is question of a Christian who took this name either for some family reason or out of devotion to St. Peter. The latter reason would not have been out of the common seeing that, in the third century, many Christians took this name so as "to be more beloved by the Saviour"

22 Th. Frankfort, in *Latomus* 20 (1961), 415-416.

— according to Dionysius of Alexandria, as reported by Eusebius.[24]

The inscription in question stirred the imagination of F. Paul Peterson, as is clear from what he writes in the booklet entitled *Peter's Tomb recently discovered in Jerusalem*.[25] A blurb summarizes the background behind the publication. Peterson was in Switzerland when he first heard talk of the tomb of St. Peter rediscovered in Jerusalem. In Rome, he consulted a book on the excavations at "Dominus Flevit," but was not satisfied with what Bagatti and Milik had written. He states expressly that the finding of the tomb of St. Peter "was deliberately concealed and that many things were lacking." Therefore, he decided to go to Jerusalem to take personal account of the whole situation. He visited "Dominus Flevit." He went to the Museum of "The Flagellation" where one can see the ossuary which had caused him such commotion. He took photos of a certain Franciscan which he also published in his work.

In his booklet he states that some Franciscans of the Holy Land had confirmed the fact that Fr. Bagatti was convinced that he had found St. Peter's tomb. According to Peterson's "romance," this was made known to Pope Pius XII who, while giving it no credence, ordered the whole business suppressed. Therefore, Peterson felt bound to make known to both Catholics and Protestants "this important find which shakes the Catholic Church to its very foundations."

Value of the discovery.

Apart from the question of the Christian character of the ossuaries, the rich discoveries opened the way to comprehensive

---

24 *Ecclesiastical History* VII, xxv, 14 (*PG* 20, 700).

25 Printed at the author's own expense. Peterson contacted Fr. Bagatti and quotes his letter in the booklet. However, he was unable to meet him in Jerusalem.

study from many angles and naturally attracted great interest. In his review of the finds, as published by Bagatti, W. F. Albright writes: "Archaeologically speaking the most important result of these excavations is the discovery of a great many ossuaries, with a wealth of decoration and with rich epigraphic material. This is certainly the most important single publication in the ossuary field. Particularly significant is the hypogeum 65-80 (p. 105) whose graffiti are the first ossuary inscriptions from Jerusalem which may be dated after A.D. 70, as was correctly emphasized by Milik." [26]

Vicente Vilar Hueso wrote a detailed review of the book in question in *Estudios Biblicos*. [27] He stated that the excavations at "Dominus Flevit" made a real contribution to our knowledge of Jewish burial grounds. The section devoted to Christian aspects of the discoveries is welcome because of its author's ability and learning. Due appreciation is made of the way in which everything is presented and illustrated. Vilar further states that when Mons. Garofalo gave news of the finds in *L'Osservatore Romano* not only the specialists, such as Bible scholars and historians were impressed, but also the general public. The reviewer deals at length with the proper names of the dead buried at "Dominus Flevit" which have a New Testament ring. He also features the Constantine monogram and the crosses, adding that, hitherto, the common opinion was that they had not been used by Christians until later times.

A Jesuit, Fr. Lebeau, reviewed a book written by a colleague, Fr. Daniélou: *Les symboles chrétiens primitifs* (Paris, 1961). He notes that the new publication is justified if only by the ossuaries found in Palestine and ascribed to the first and second centuries. They bear the symbols which Daniélou, on the basis of literary com-

---

26   W. F. Albright, in *Bulletin of the American Schools of Oriental Research*, no. 159, October, 1960, 37.

27   V. Vilar Hueso, "Onomástica neotestamentaria y símbolos cristianos en el cemeterio de 'Dominus Flevit'," in *Estúdios Bíblicos* 18 (1959), 285-291.

parisons, had already interpreted as Jewish Christian. Lebeau adds that some of the photos in the appendix which were sent to him confirm the conclusions reached in the book under review. Besides, Daniélou, in the introduction to this work (p. 8), does not conceal his great satisfaction that others, working along different lines, had reached the same conclusions as himself. [28]

The "Dominus Flevit" discoveries were of great interest to the daily press also. Thus, amongst other items, a letter, with an appropriate reply, was published in the local Israeli daily *The Jerusalem Post*. The request for information on the discovery of a Jewish Christian cemetery on Olivet was addressed to the paper on June 14, 1960, bearing the name of M. Feverstein of Ramat Gan. The reply was published in the same paper on July 6, 1960. The writer was Dr. P. P. Kahane, Director of the Jerusalem Museum and temporary Director of Antiquities in the Ministry of Education and Culture in Israel. Kahane referred to the book by Bagatti and Milik dealing with the subject. He added that in "this book there is a description of a number of ossuaries which bear what the authors suppose to be Christian symbols." It is evident that Kahane was careful to avoid passing any judgment on the matter.

Jack Finegan, in his volume *The Archaeology of the New Testament* [28a], after having examined with particular care the epigraphic findings of the ossuaries, concludes: "With respect to the items which have now been shown from Dominus flevit (Nos. 273-279) it is of interest to note that many of the signs which are capable of Christian interpretation and many of the names which are also known in the NT come from the group of burial place N° 79... Where there are, thus, signs that can be Christian, and names that are frequent or prominent in NT and therefore might

---

28 P. Lebeau, in *Nouvelle Revue Théologique* 94 (1962), 649.
28a Princeton, New Jersey 1969, pp. 100-101, 243-249.

have been preferred by Christians, it surely comes within the realm of possibility that at least this area in particular is a burial place of Jewish families some of whose members had become Christians". Finegan's study of "Dominus Flevit" is included as part of his whole study of the entire literature and the allied monuments.

2. *The excavations at Nazareth.*

An atmosphere of dismay and doubt.

In 1620, the Custody of the Holy Land got possession of the shrine of the Annunciation at Nazareth. A church built there in the eighteenth century had become inadequate for the needs of the increasing numbers of parishioners and pilgrims. So, in 1955, the Custody began work on a new basilica which would both answer these needs and restore to the place its original splendour. This was also an opportunity for archaeological excavations, and they were directed by Bagatti. At the start, prospects were anything but promising. Some scholars had, shall we say, vied in demolishing the genuineness of the tradition which sited the place of the mysteries of the Annunciation and Incarnation there. Arguments against the authenticity of the tradition in question were drawn from history and archaeology. In the event, all this was proven worthless.

For example, some scholars selected as their basis of attack a text in St. Epiphanius in which he states that the Jews of Nazareth had prevented "Christians" from dwelling there in the first four centuries. [29] Hence the conclusion that it was impossible to hold the old tradition about Nazareth. Gaston Le Hardy wrote: "The history of Nazareth in the second century comes down to the sad fact that the enemies of Christ were its sole proprietors." [30]

---

[29] Cfr. B. Bagatti, *Gli scavi di Nazaret*, I. Jerusalem, 1967, 16-17.
[30] G. Le Hardy, *Histoire de Nazareth et de ses sanctuaires*. Paris, 1905, 18.

The following year, Ulisse Chevalier added : "The Jews obtained the privilege of not allowing anyone to live amongst them who was not of their own religion. In these circumstances, it is very unlikely that material monuments to the Incarnation could have been preserved there. Thus it is that the first pilgrims seem to have been ignorant of the Holy Places in Galilee. [31]

Such claims were made in the name of unexamined documents and contrary to information provided in Eusebius' Ecclesiastical History wherein he tells us that the relatives of Jesus lived on in Nazareth. Working on false premises, some writers proceeded to demolish the tradition attached to one of the most important shrines. However, we shall see later what exactly Epiphanius meant when he spoke of the "Christians."

Other writers used archaeology to the same end. Though neither Bible scholar nor archaeologist, the German priest, Clemens Kopp, wrote against the genuineness of the Nazareth sanctuary. He came to the Holy Land as a refugee from Nazism and settled on Carmel. He wrote up the history of that site, then focused his attention on Nazareth. [32]

Dealing with the shrine of the Annunciation, he took as his basis the reports of some author that tombs had been found in the locality. He concluded that the sanctuary must therefore be conceived as built over a cemetery in Christian times. Thus, the whole thing is to be regarded as a "pia fraus." Because of the richness of his material, and the scientific way in which he wrote it up, many scholars accepted Kopp's conclusions without further reference to other sources.

Canon R. Leconte wrote in this connection : "The lack of exact information about the place where the Holy Family would have

---

31   U. Chevalier, *Notre-Dame de Lorette*. Paris, 1906, 21.
32   C. Kopp, "Beiträge zur Geschichte Nazareths," in *The Journal of the Palestine Oriental Society* 18 (1938), 187-228; 19 (1941), 82-119; 253-285.

lived has been compensated for by the pious imaginings of the faithful. Around the town, they tended to find more and more sanctuaries. Here, the Madonna would have lived at the time of the Annunciation, there she would have brought up the child Jesus. Every locality has its sacred places. But, these diggings, these buildings, these mosaics go back only to a recent period, to the Byzantine at the earliest. They were connected with an area which was situated on the edge of first-century Nazareth and which served as a burial ground. No Jew would have dreamed of making his home there for fear of contracting some legal impurity." [33] Leconte tells us how, subsequently he was led up the hill to where the Salesian residence and the adjoining workshops are situated. There he remained satisfied and content.

Clarification by excavation.

It was in this atmosphere which was affecting scholars more and more that the archaeological diggings at Nazareth were begun. Joyful is the only expression to use of their reaction when, soon after work began, the archaeologists found that the famous tombs on which Kopp had based his "pia fraus" theory just did not exist. Instead, remains of a Byzantine church came to light, together with underground corridors leading to granaries, storerooms, etc.

The various archaeological schools of Palestine were officially invited to view the finds and to acquaint themselves with all the details. Following such a visit, Benoit of the Ecole Biblique wrote that, while the Crusader church was already well known, the Byzantine building "has recently been found, thanks to the excavations by Fr. Bagatti, O.F.M. They are still unfinished but they are sufficient to allow of a reconstruction of the plan of the primitive monument. The Reverend Father will, in time, publish a complete

32   R. Leconte, *Jérusalem et les Lieux-saints*. Paris, 1954, 30.

Fig. 16. During the Excavations in Nazareth, in the zone of the Annunciation. (From *Scavi di Nazaret*, p. 135).

and scientific account of the new excavations. The observations I am making now are deliberately general.... This area is perforated by silos and cisterns. It offers Roman-Byzantine pottery, beginning with the first century after Christ — evidence of a long occupation of the locality which corresponds very well with Nazareth of the Gospels. This area does not have any tombs, as was at one time stated." [34]

Benoit's very prudent observations tended to lift from scholars' minds the impressions which resulted from Kopp's too hasty conclusions. However, in all fairness, we must immediately add that, subsequently, Kopp himself in his book on the Holy Places (trans-

---

[34] P. Benoit, "La nouvelle église de l'Annonciation à Nazareth," in *La vie intellectuelle*, June 1955, 26-28.

lated into many languages) modified his statements by taking into account the results of the archaeological excavations. [35] So, also, Leconte took occasion of the diggings to announce to readers of *Bible et Terre Sainte* the discoveries at Nazareth. Thus, in a report on the excavations, he writes : "Let us simply recall that controversies arose about the most important of all (the sanctuaries). The recent excavations by Fr. Bagatti have put an end to these." [36]

The other argument which had been used by scholars in rejecting the genuineness of the traditional shrine of the Annunciation was drawn from St. Epiphanius. According to him, the Jews were accustomed to hinder the "Christians" from dwelling in Nazareth. The hitherto common interpretation of this was demolished by the archaeological finds. This came about through the discovery of a pre-Byzantine church and through a philological examination of the word "Christian." The latter showed that, in the third and fourth centuries, the term designated the faithful of Gentile origin only and was not applied to the Judaeo-Christians who had always remained in the locality with their own properties, thus keeping intact the traditions relative to the shrines of the town.

Some details of the excavation.

For a better understanding of the results of the Nazareth excavations, we must go into some detail. The interested reader will find still fuller and more thoroughly documented reports in Bagatti's first volume *Gli scavi di Nazaret,* I. (Jerusalem : Franciscan Press, 1967).

With a view to setting it on a new bed, the mosaic pavement of the Byzantine church was taken up. Digging continued in order to reach the virgin rock and also to avoid leaving any impression

---

35   C. Kopp, *Die heiligen Stätten der Evangelien.* Regensburg, 1959, 86-129.
36   R. Leconte, in *Bible et Terre Sainte,* no. 7 (1958), 8-10.

that the excavation had not been complete. This yen for thorough-ness was once more rewarded by the discovery of some stones coated with wash, quite similar to the ancient synagogues of Galilee. The remains of a wall and of painted decoration confirmed the existence of a building older than the Byzantine church.

The many graffiti which came to light show that the place was frequented and venerated by the faithful of many nationalities. This is clear from the inscriptions in various tongues. Three graffiti are worthy of special mention. In the first are to be seen the letters XE MAPIA: "Hail Mary," an invocation of the Madonna which is of particular interest for the site and its period. There is question of an inscription which is older than the Council of Ephesus (431). Besides arguing in favour of the authenticity of the shrine, it also furnishes a proof that Mary was venerated at a very early time, prior to the Council.

A second graffito speaks of the "holy place of M." (probably the first letter of "Mary" and of the "image of her." This second find attests worship of Mary in this locality. Finally, there is a third inscription on marble. According to Testa, who studied it, the words recall a *targum* (commentary) on Isaiah (55:1 and 13) which, if not referring directly to the Madonna at least makes reference to the Incarnation of the Word through the exegetical theory which views "the wells" as fountains of grace. [37] Thus, the diggings at Nazareth, begun under the most discouraging circumstances, have provided the most positive proof of the genuineness of the shrine. It is now the most richly documented of all, so far as archaeology is concerned.

The same excavations have also meant much for the history of the Judaeo-Christians. It is now beyond all doubt that the shrine

---

37   E. Testa, "Il Targum di Isaia 55, 1. 13 scoperte a Nazaret e la Teologia sui pozzi dell'Acqua Viva." in *LA* 17 (1967), 259-289. "L'apporto delle iscri-zioni nazaretane," in *Rivista Biblica* 16 (1968), 167-185.

was in their hands. It was they who frequented it, venerated it and carried on their particular kind of worship there.

Further, the scholars from the Franciscan House of Biblical Studies were able to compare the symbols found around Nazareth with those discovered on the ossuaries of "Dominus Flevit' and other places. It was established that they were identical, and this provided another argument in favour of the Christian character of the latter. In other words, seeing that the symbols at Nazareth could be ascribed to Christians only, it followed that those on the ossuaries and tombs (some quite similar to those at Nazareth, some obviously belonging to the same current of tradition) must also be ascribed to Christians.

As is well known, the archaeological work at Nazareth went on for some twelve years. Thus, the first successful campaign was followed by a task calling for much patience while the new basilica was being constructed. Digging had to be done gradually according as building operations allowed of excavations near the sacred grotto itself. Each discovery was made known to scholars through articles in *La Terra Santa* and *L'Osservatore Romano*.

The definitive publication of results.

Bagatti waited long and patiently before sending his first volume on the excavations to the press. The delay was the more prolonged in view of the pressure put on him by many to finish more quickly. Only when the workmen had laid down their picks and all hope of further finds became improbable (seeing that all had already been explored) was Bagatti able to bring all the results together for peaceful study and examination. For some twelve years, the bulk of his type-script remained in his desk. From time to time he took it out to make the additions and finer touches dictated by the later finds. [38]

In this book, the author did not aim to state a proposition. His sole purpose was to set out, as clearly as possible, the material which had been found. Knowing well that his fellow archaeologists wanted to see with their own eyes before committing themselves, he not only provided sketches of the more important discoveries but also photos and, quite often, enlargements. The conclusions flowing from a study of all the material will certainly be drawn by the experts. Bagatti has sought simply to establish the various chronological stages of the monument and to present each report in its proper time-setting.

Nevertheless, it is clear, even to one less informed on detailed Jewish Christian questions, that the Nazareth discoveries have provided new elements which have bearing on this subject. Amongst the obvious conclusions, for instance, is that of the duration of Jewish Christian presence at the shrine of Nazareth. From the graffiti and monuments, it is evident that it extended to the end of the fifth century. No one will miss the importance of such evidence. It is the more valuable seeing that we were able to glean only vague hints on the matter from the written sources.

3. *The funerary symbols of Khirbet Kilkish.*

Clandestine diggings.

In 1960, a vendor of antiquities, M. Beidun, who has a shop on the Via Dolorosa between the Fifth and Sixth Stations of the Cross, Jerusalem, showed scholars from "The Flagellation" a stele

---

38 B. Bagatti, *Gli scavi di Nazaret*. Volume I: *Dalle origini al secolo XII*. Jerusalem, 1967. pp.vii-316, with 9 Plates. At the request of scholars an English translation was made: Eugene Hoade, O.F.M., *Excavations in Nazareth*. Jerusalem, 1969.

of rather soft stone on which there were to be seen many symbols of various shapes : crosses, birds and, amongst the other details, seven lines in the form of steps. Therein, Fr. Testa discerned elements of the "cosmic ladder" mentioned in books written in the early centuries under Jewish Christian influence. Through Fr. Augustus Spijkerman, director of the Museum of "The Flagellation," the stele was purchased and today it can be viewed in the Museum together with other items acquired later. On all of them, Fr. Testa detected quite rare themes which could be explained only by reference to Jewish Christian teaching and, especially, that of the Arcontics.

Some scholars, completely unacquainted with the doctrinal heritage of the Judaeo-Christians, were puzzled by the novelty of so many different items hitherto unknown. Some were inclined to think of "a fraud." However, there could be no real doubt seeing that the material was so abundant and so well preserved. Nevertheless, light had to be thrown on many things, especially on the matter of origin and dating. This latter consideration urged the professors of "The Flagellation" to ask the antiquarian to show them other objects which had been found together with the symbols. He produced items of pottery dating from the late Roman period. Subsequently, the accuracy of this dating was vindicated when the scholars were able to view an abundance of such pottery on the very site where the stele-symbols had been found.

Getting to know something of the origin of these particular finds was a more complicated problem for the experts. This was due especially to the background of connivance which was found to lie behind the whole matter. The man who had originally produced the objects had come across some of them by chance and had not informed the Department of Antiquities. He was afraid of police action and asked Beidun, the antiquarian of Via Dolorosa to whom he had sold them, not to tell where they had come from.

It was then that the scholars, searching their memories, re-

Fig. 17.   The hill of Kilkish from the north. (From *LTS* 1964, p. 265).

called that, at one time, in the vicinity of Hebron, a certain Peter had founded a small community of faithful called the Arcontics, with whom St. Eusebius had done battle. [39]

One day, Fr. Bagatti went to the shop in question and, putting on a bolder front than he really felt, firmly stated that he knew that the objects had originated around Hebron. Thinking that he was discovered, the antiquarian did not argue but agreed to accompany Fr. Spijkerman to the spot. On February 12, 1961, both went to Khirbet Kilkish. There, Fr. Spijkerman asked one Mohammed Dasan el-Rifai, the owner of the field in which the stones had been

[39]   *Adv. Haereses* I, III, 40 (*PG* 41, 677-692).

74

unearthed, to dig in three different places in succession. In all three, at a depth of about eighty centimetres, some kind of marked stone was found.

Genuineness of the items found.

Efforts to arrive at certainty did not stop there. Some time later, the Franciscan archaeologists Bagatti, Testa and Corbo, under

Fig. 18. The clandestine excavator intervewed
(From *LTS* 1964, p. 266)

the guidance of Fr. Spijkerman, returned to the spot to take personal note of the place and the finds made there. They noted that the field was partially tilled, partially uncultivated, and that it was surrounded by a wall which held a certain interest because it was very old. They saw that some ancient dressed stones had been collected on the site to provide the owner with materials for building a small house. They also saw that, in one corner of the field, there was a large deposit of ceramics similar to that already examined in Jerusalem. Other pieces were scattered here and there, some embedded in the soil of the field.

The Fathers had taken along about twenty photos of the pieces kept in the Museum of "The Flagellation," and they showed them to Mohammed Dasan el-Rifai. He immediately recognized them and offered to point out the exact spot where he had found them. Before leaving, the scholars purchased other pieces directly from the owner of the field. This unwittingly provoked the displeasure of Nasser ed-Din and of Abu Suleiman Rasas, two antiquarians of Hebron who claimed the monopoly of sales of steles found at Khirbet Kilkish.

The scholars' visit, their conversation with the finder of the items, his immediate reaction to the pictures of what he had found and sold, the naturalness and spontaneity of his answers — all confiirmed the genuineness of the finds. We need hardly add that, within a short time, requests for stones from Khirbet Kilkish came in from different centres of study. They were sought after especially for the inscriptions and designs they bore. With regard to the latter, we should state immediately that they are in a popular style, without artistic pretension.

For some time, the stones were continually on sale and several people were interested in buying them. Amongst others, we remember Dr. Licinio Vestri, Italian Vice-Consul who kindly allowed the scholars from "The Flagellation" to make sketches and photos of those in his collection. Similar permission was granted by others: Mr. Mario Tonarelli, Italian Consul General in Jerusalem and U.N.O. Colonels P. Gregori, A. Emmanuelli, P. Troiani and A. Annése of Italy, and John Tee of Australia.

In the meantime, Dasan el-Rifai realized that he could make more profit from the stones by by-passing the middle-men of Hebron. He went to Jerusalem but, in doing so, gave offense to Nasser ed-Din who claimed that he had acquired the right to make all sales, especially as he had been instrumental in getting Mohammed Dasan el-Rifai out of jail where he had been confined on account of his clandestine diggings.

76

Because much of this detail was unknown, and because of the nature of certain publications on the subject, some scholars still hesitated about the authenticity of the funerary steles discovered at Khirbet Kilkish. [40] Moreover, a find of this kind is not quite

Fig. 19. Some amulets of Kh. Kilkish (From *LTS*. 1960, p. 236).

unique. Designs on glass similar to those found on the Khirbet Kilkish steles have come to light, as also objects recovered at Tell Minnis in Syria. More striking is the similarity between the great mass of material found at Kh. Rizqeh, east of Akaba, and the items from Kh. Kilkish. Diana Kirkbride [41] has an accurate report on the two seasons of diggings at Kh. Rizqeh. She states that about three hundred stones were found representing male and female subjects. Some of the items are damaged or chipped, others are whole.

The likenesses to the Kh. Kilkish material is evident from (a) designs done in abstract style ; (b) discovery of material in an

---

40   Cfr. R. Le Déaut, in *Biblica* 47 (1966), 283, note; L. Randellini, in *Studi Francescani* 64 (1967), 11.

41   D. Kirkbride, in *RB* 67 (1960), 232-235; and in "Ancient Arabian Ancestor Idols," *Archaeology* 22 (1969), 116-121.

Fig. 20. Two amulets with the sign of a triangle. (From *LTS* 1964, p. 266)

Fig. 21. Dolls found at Kh. Rizquel in Transjordan (From *Archaeology*, 1969, p. 120)

enclosed place ; (c) forms of the steles ; (d) the frequency of a certain relief in the work ; (e) the encounter of the same doctrinal current of religious ideas. The only difference which might be stressed is that the material found at Kh. Kilkish is richer from the theological viewpoint. Clearly, it points to a more developed type of religion.

Subsequently, Fr. Bagatti was asked by other scholars to return several times to Kh. Kilkish. On June 24, 1964, Dr. Vestri took a photo of the excavator. [42] On May 15, 1967, Fr. Bagatti pointed out the place to two Protestant scholars. He asserts that on these visits he failed to see the least trace of deception or fraud. Mohammed Dasan el-Rifai stated that he had nothing more to show or sell. Yet, we know that various items in stone are still in the possession of the antiquarian, Beidun, and of Nasser ed-Din. Also, the latter still has the fourth-century coins found together with the stones.

Some scholars are still trying to decipher the inscriptions on the stones but, so far, nothing has been published. Many of the stone-designs have been edited by Testa, [43] many others have yet to be made known to the public. The experts hope to be able to decipher them, seeing that many of the steles are inter-related and show continuous script. Once the writings have been translated, there is no doubt that a book dealing with all the material found will be published.

42 B. Bagatti, in *LTS* 40 (1964), 264-269. The photograph of the excavator is reproduced. I myself have been able to view the field within the ancient wall, and I know that the shaped stones came from there and not from elsewhere.

43 E. Testa, *ISGC*, 95-114.

4. *The millenarian tomb and the ossuaries of Bethphage.*

During the excavations conducted through 1949-1953, at Bethany, under the direction of Silvester Saller, in the property of the Custody of the Holy Land, some material relative to Bethphage was also found. Because of the closeness of the two places, and the similarity

Fig. 22. Entrance to millenarian tomb of Bethphage (From *LA* XI, p. 239)

of the material dug up, Saller planned to describe both localities in one book. However, the volume on Bethany grew so large that he decided to deal with Bethphage separately. [44]

In this latter area, the property of the Custody of the Holy Land, various tombs of the Roman period came to light. Saller and the archaeologists of "The Flagellation" inspected the tombs found previously or during the past few years and were particularly interested in one in the form of an *arcosolium*. Its entrance was closed by a round stone and, within, the grave was marked by inscriptions and symbols. Comparing these latter with those already known, the scholars had to admit that the writings in this tomb were foreign to them and that, seemingly, they had not been used elsewhere.

Testa set about examining this grave and, as often, he made a comparison with Jewish Christian teaching already familiar to him. He finally succeeded in giving an explanation of the symbols. Some he interpreted in the light of beliefs in Millenarianism which was in fashion during the first centuries of the Christian era, especially in Jerusalem. Others he compared with Jewish Christian beliefs in the future life or in the journey which the soul had to undertake to gain heaven, the journey symbolized by the "cosmic ladder" sketched in the tomb itself.

Saller made use of this work by Testa [45] and, putting it into English, inserted it into his study of the locality. [46]

The discovery did not cause too much surprise seeing that, in 1910, in the same property of the Custody, a tomb containing ossuaries had been found by Brother Luke Thoennessen. He made a

---

44   S. Saller, *Excavations at Bethany* (1949-1953). Jerusalem, 1957.
45   E. Testa, "The Graffiti of Tomb 21 at Bethphage," in *LA* 11 (1960-1961), 251-287.
46   S. Saller, "The Archaeological Setting of the Shrine of Bethphage," in *LA* 11 (1960-1961), 172-250, and then Vol. I of the "Minor" Collection of the Franciscan House of Biblical Studies.

Fig. 23. Graffiti on the wall of the room. (From *LA* XI, p. 254)

sketch of the plan of the tomb and drew the ossuaries. Later, the Franciscan archaeologist, Fr. Gaudenzio Orfali, illustrated these finds, making use of the design done by his confrere. [47]

One of the ossuaries described by Orfali was closed by a lid on which proper names could be read. Orfali interpreted them as those of the deceased. Some of these names were accompanied by some kind of title such as "Galilean." This led Saller to think of the possibility that a colony of Galileans had once lived in the place. As he himself implies, this would explain how easy it was for Jesus to come by his mount just before the triumphal entry into Jerusalem.

Studying the archaeological material relative to the early centuries of Christianity, Testa took account of the lids of the two ossuaries. One was taken to the Louvre, the other is kept in the museum of "The Flagellation." Regarding this latter, Testa was able to examine it at ease, even using chemical procedures which allowed him to discover other letters covered by a kind of incrustation. This process, besides permitting easier reading, made it possible for him to establish the genuineness of the material which had been called in question by scholars because they were unfamiliar with the nature of the inscriptions. [48]

Testa interprets the list of names engraved on the ossuaries in the light of the ancient practice which is still in use in Egypt. The deceased are remembered by calling them by name ("The Book of Life"). Consolation for the living is sought by means of this com-

---

47 G. Orfali, "Un hypogée juif à Bethphagé," in *RB* 32 (1923), 253-260.

48 There is question here of W. F. Albright (in *Journal of Biblical Literature* 56 (1937), 157ff.) and of J. T. Milik (cfr. *Gli scavi del 'Dominus Flevit'*, p. 187.) Brother Luke was an expert on antiquities and, amongst other things, he directed the excavations of the medieval church at Gethsemane. Cfr. V. Corbo, *Ricerche archeologiche al Monte degli Ulivi*. Jerusalem, 1951. It would be hard to conceive of his putting a false item in the museum and giving the genuine one away.

memoration and it is thought to aid the dead also. Testa interprets the numbers attached to the names as part of the symbolism associated with the ceremony. [49] René Dessaud, who had studied the lid of the ossuary in the Museum of the Louvre had taken them to be sums of payments due. [50]

5. *The mosaic of Bet ha-Šitta.*

At the foot of the hill which, to the north, blocks off the plain in front of Beisan, quite close to Kibbutz Bet ha-Šitta, there was found an unusual collection of structures consisting of eight rooms and a press. Two of the rooms had mosaic floors, but their patterns were quite rare. Instead of the usual Graeco-Roman motifs, there were to be seen designs consisting of very rough symbols, almost shapeless, with letters drawn haphazardly. In one room, there was a cross in mosaic, apparently surrounded by scrolls.

The Israeli archaeologists who dealt with the discovery put scholars in touch with it. Y. Aharoni, in charge of the digging, submitted the official report, [51] and Avi-Yonah hinted at it during the Fifth Congress of Christian Archaeology. [52] They dealt with the differences between these mosaics and those known already. They also made a close study of the letters and symbols found in the locality. They concluded that there was question of a Christian building.

Testa followed on with a detailed examination, aiming to fix

---

49   E. Testa, *ISGC*, 211-222.
50   R. Dussaud, "Comptes d'ouvriers d'une entreprise funéraire juive," in *Syria* 4 (1923), 241-249.
51   Y. Aharoni, "Excavations at Beth-Hashitta," in *Bulletin of the Israel Exploration Society* 18 (1954), 209-215.
52   M. Avi-Yonah, in *Actes du Ve Congrès International d'Archéologie chrétienne*, Vatican City-Paris 1957, 122.

and interpret the details of the mosaic of Bet ha-Šitta. He studied all the symbols over again and, noting both the literary data and the ancient Oriental ways of expression, was able to give an explanation of it all, relating it to a fuller development of the sign of the "cosmic ladder." [53].

The mosaic panel in the floor of one room shows it fully. The frame round about it is fashioned in the form of steps. Inside, the various stages of heaven, with their different characteristics, are represented, and all is crowned with the symbols of divine dwellings. Testa's interpretation gives meaning not only to one or other symbol but to the whole presentation. We must take it that the motifs are not isolated and haphazard, but that they were conceived and executed by the artist following one sole master-idea.

The floor of the two rooms showed a development of the theme of the life to come, with Christ as the last end. Here there are brought together all the different ideas on the "cosmic ladder" and on the various forms thereof. These had already been met with in numerous documents and monuments, as well as in the symbols engraved on tombs and ossuaries. It offered the further advantage of showing the links which exist between them.

Dealing with the discovery, Avi-Yonah had written: "The date of this agricultural installation is much discussed." [54] He was, indeed, right. The fact that a cross was designed on the floor would suggest that the date of the establishment was prior to 427 or later than 614. The first figure is indicated by the fact that, in 427, Emperor Theodosius had forbidden the placing of crosses on pavements. The latter date represents the end of the domination of Christian emperors in the region. The very rough style of execution would also, perhaps, suggest the later date.

53   E. Testa, in *ISGC*, 84-92.
54   M. Avi-Yonah, *loc. cit.*

With a view to trying to fix the time more precisely, the scholars of "The Flagellation" decided to visit the place and to seek some traces of pottery. This element is not mentioned in Aharoni's report. To their great surprise, they found that everything had been removed. The main panel, if we can call it that, which features the "cosmic ladder" now serves as the floor of an open pool in Jerusalem. The design with the cross was, unfortunately, not to be found anywhere.

Yet, fixing the date is of relative importance for we know that the Judaeo-Christians lived on long after the coming of the Christian emperors. To explain why such mosaics are different from the usual, we can only suggest that the designers had no contact either with pagan artists or with Christians of Gentile stock. This possibility was also put forward in the case of the ossuaries and the mosaic found at Khirbet Siyar el-Ghanam, near Bethlehem. [55]

6. *The lamella of the Oil of Faith.*

As we have seen in the first chapter, museums possess many ancient lamellae. They consist of all kinds of material: lead, copper, bronze, silver and gold. On some, only designs are to be seen, on others, only inscriptions. Finally, some have both. Usually, they contain magical formulae, composed of different letters of the alphabet and ornamented with other strange symbols. A few show traces of numbers. All these elements remind us somewhat of the cabbala (mystic interpretation in Jewish oral tradition).

Generally, the lamellae are difficult to understand because the designer has deliberately left them obscure. He wished that only the initiated would grasp their sense. All this has resulted in schol-

55 V. Corbo, *Gli scavi di Kh. Siyar el-Ghanam (Campo dei Pastori) e i monasteri dei dintorni.* Jerusalem, 1955, 40-41; photos 49-50.

Fig. 24. Lamella of "Oil
of Faith"
(From *L'Huile*, p.22).

ars taking slight interest in them, not wanting to spend time and energy on the study and editing of this kind of discovery — the more so, seeing that there is question of amulets which seem to have little scientific value.

As noted, the Museum of "The Flagellation" has a silver lamella, originating in Aleppo. It had already been published by Schwab. Testa turned his attention to it again for he was not satisfied with Schwab's interpretation. He re-examined the lettering and sought the true meaning. The conclusion he reached is that this lamella, too, reflects Judaeo-Christian teaching.

Encouraged by these results, Testa took up the study of the Beirut lamella already examined by Dupont-Sommer. This, too, can easily be set within the same framework of ideas and given its right interpretation. Subsequently, Testa turned his attention to the Amwas lamella, published by Père Vincent, and once again he reached a positive conclusion, namely, one which is logical, harmonious with the ancient texts and parallel to other archaeological finds in the same locality. An identical method is followed in all cases. The literary texts help explain the artefact, while the latter provides an interpretation of the former. [56]

His familiarity with lamellae and his ability to compare one with another has made it fairly easy for Testa to distinguish the various currents of thought contained therein, as also to distinguish an amulet from a lamella which manifests orthodox teaching.

It was this background of training and experience which enabled him to recognize the importance and value of a lamella which the antiquarian, Mr. Beidun showed Fr. Saller who was passing his shop on Via Dolorosa in January, 1963. The shopkeeper said that some Beduin had brought it to him. Terra-cotta lamps found in the same locality were also produced. The combination of the Aramaic lamella

---

[56] E. Testa, *ISGC*, 52-66.

with the Herodian-type lamps, obviously from the first century A.D., stirred Saller's interest. He spoke of it enthusiastically to his confreres at "The Flagellation." Fr. Spijkerman visited the antiquarian and succeeded in bringing the lamella back to "The Flagellation" for a preliminary examination. This was carried out by Fr. Testa who immediately insisted that the object be bought. He set about acquiring the funds necessary for the purchase and this was finally effected by Fr. Spijkerman.

On translating the text, Fr. Testa immediately sensed its connection with the rite of anointing described in St. James (Jas 5:14-15) and gave news of it in a brief report published in *L'Osservatore Romano*, later reprinted in *La Terra Santa*. [57]

The truly sensational announcement by Testa caused great surprise and brought varying reactions from scholars. Some immediately asked for a fuller explanation and, on receiving it, agreed with Testa's interpretation. Others remained sceptical; some scoffed.

The definitive publication of results.

The unfavorable reactions were, shall we say, somewhat impulsive and did not disturb Testa at all. He had the precious document in his hands and he proceeded to study it more deeply from both the epigraphical and exegetical angles. Following four years of thought and research on the subject, he published an exhaustive study in French, the translator and adapter being the noted man of letters, Omer Englebert. [58]

---

57 E. Testa, "Scoperta del Primitivo Rito della Estrema Unzione in una Laminella del I secolo," in *L'Osservatore Romano*, February 8, 1963; and in *LTS* 39 (1963), 70-74.

58 E. Testa, *L'Huile de la foi. L'Onction des malades sur une lamelle du Ier siècle*. Translated and adapted from the Italian by Omer Englebert. Jerusalem, 1967. Pp. 136.

First, Testa examined the text on the lamella from the viewpoint of palaeography. J. C. Picard, a Protestant scholar, praised the well-documented analysis. [59] This thorough examination warranted Testa in claiming that the inscription on the lamella goes back to 70-80 A.D. Subsequent to this study, the author went on to describe the lamella and to propose two translations, one literal and one free. Regarding this translation, Picard says: "It is based on a very detailed philological exegesis and on a commentary which summarizes quite strikingly, but also quite handily, the free translation." Again, he states that Testa's study was conducted "in masterly fashion and the criticisms which can be made here and there do not, in our opinion, put the essential conclusion in danger...."

Picard is convinced, and he says so more than once, that the interpretation is right. There is question of a ritual anointing. Through this a man who, because of his blindness and stupidity, has fallen into a ditch prepared by the angel Qur'el ("he who digs ditches, wells"), may take hope that his suffering will be alleviated and that, while he is being cured, he will also obtain pardon of his sins by God. To bring about this happy result, it is first necessary that the patient be "examined in the Name," that is, questioned about his faults. Then, he is to be sprinkled with oil by means of "a twig" shaken over him. In the inscription, there follows a reminder that there is no need to have recourse to an offerer of sacrifices as in the Old Testament. Lines 12-14 recall the benefits of the sprinkling: the trial is alleviated, and the "blindness and indebtedness of the foolish person are forgiven." In addition, as Picard notes, the administration of the sacrament implies "the forgiveness of sins," as in the Epistle of James.

Testa queried whether the lamella should be listed with the

---

59   J.-C. Picard, "L'Huile de la foi," in *La Terre Sainte*, 1967, 150-152. Italian translation in *LTS* 43 (1967), 131-135. (Review of Fr. Testa's book.)

90

other symbols and replied that this one has nothing to do with amulets. It is to be considered a kind of "laissez-passer" which will serve Qur'el's victim well in his ascent of the "cosmic ladder." This passport would be designed to prove that the former patient had received the sacred rite of aspersion, with its resultant effect of the forgiveness of sins.

The little document, measuring 60 cm. by 24, is of great importance. As Picard says, Testa's study is fundamental at present for it is not only the work of a skilled historian-philologue but also of a theologian quite conversant with tradition.

In the preface to his book on the subject, Testa ends with an invitation to scholars to busy themselves with the few points which still remain obscure and, in detail, with the symbols of line 9 together with the text in lines 14b-16 which he was unable to reconstruct exactly. In anticipation, he offers his congratulations to anyone who can achieve an interpretation before him.

Milik's intervention.

J. T. Milik immediately took up Testa's invitation.[60] However, he aimed, not only to decipher the symbols of line 9 and the hidden meaning of lines 14b-16 but to present his own fascimile of the whole lamella, fashioned from the photos published in *L'Huile de la Foi*. This reconstruction differs considerably from that made by Testa from the original. As a result, Milik's translation is completely different from Testa's. In Milik's version, the sacramental rite of the sick is not even hinted at. Therefore, the lamella is simply *a Jewish Christian amulet* of very little importance. This precisely is the title given by Milik to his criticism of *L'Huile de la Foi*.

60 J. T. Milik, "Une amulette judéo-araméenne," in *Biblica* 48 (1967), 450-451.

Fig. 25. Lamella of "Oil of faith", according to the transcription of fr. Testa (from *L'Huile*, p. 13)

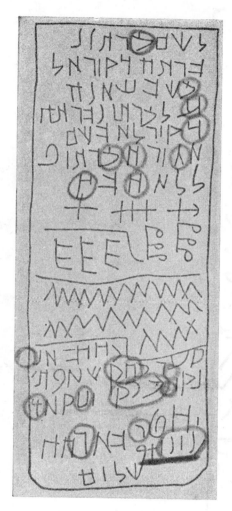

Fig. 26. Lamella of "Oil of Faith" according to the transcription of Milik, with annotations showing the non-correspondence with the original of fr. Testa. (From LTS 1968, p. 57)

First, he sums up Testa's work in two lines and a half, tagging it a "curious publication." Then he states: "This is how I read and interpret this small text of magical invocation. The reading of lines 1-7 seems quite accurate. Regarding the second part, that is, lines 12-16, it would be necessary to view the object itself again (*revoir*), since the surface of the lamella is very much damaged here." Then there follows the translation which agrees with that of Testa in only three or four words. After some remarks of a technical nature, aimed at justifying the reading and the translation, Milik ends, "By comparing my reading and translation with those of the author of *L'Huile de la Foi* one can see that, out of some thirty words, only three of four have been deciphered correctly. And, since a correct or nearly correct deciphering is an essential condition for any study resulting from it, the reflections on the various subjects found in Testa's book are meaningless." [61]

For myself, I must confess that I read and re-read the opening and closing lines of this article several times. I did it to make sure whether or not my first impressions were well founded. However, the painful feeling remained, namely, that Milik's criticism is decidedly sinister. I thought there must be some other reason for this kind of critique.

As a matter of fact, when studying certain parts of Testa's huge work *Il simbolismo dei Giudeo-cristiani*, I found that he had quite plainly contradicted Milik several times. One instance was the question of the genuineness of an ossuary discovered at Bethphage. Milik had declared it spurious but Testa, on the contrary, had proven it genuine. Again, regarding another Bethphage ossuary, marked with names and numerals, Milik had interpreted it "as wages for workmen." Testa, meanwhile, viewed it as representing invocations in favour of the dead. [62]

Milik's destructive criticism drew an early reply from Testa. Aided by friends, he immediately sent scholars who were particularly interested two mimeographed pages in which he pointed out that Milik had forged fifteen letters; others he had added; some

---

61 *Idem, art. cit.*, 451.
62 E. Testa, *ISGC*, 135-136, 213.

94

Fig. 27. Lamella of "Oil of Faith": new photograph (upper part)

he had removed. Testa remarked: "To reconstruct a fascimile without ever having seen the document is not quite scientific and is often dangerous, both with regard to the transcription and the translation. Trying to criticize our work, the noted palaeographer, J. T.

Milik, has fallen into this trap." Testa went on to make a criticism of each letter which Milik had forged, added or removed.

Regarding the date of the lamella, Testa confidently traces it back to the first century. Milik, very hesitantly, ascribes it to the fifth or sixth century and does not exclude even the High Middle Ages. On this Testa remarks: "Finally, it is strange that a palaeo-

Fig. 28. New photograph with the detail (lower part) of the disputed letters.

grapher who has dated fragments of three or four letters found at Qumran with extreme exactness, has not succeeded of late in dating at least seven lines, the reading of which he has judged 'quite certain.' Once he does hazard a guess, it is difficult to understand how he can swing between the fifth century and the Middle Ages."

Testa remarks that Milik had never seen the original document. This is contrary to what Milik could be taken to mean when he writes "It is necessary to view the object itself again (*revoir*)." "In fine, to achieve his facsimile, Milik has worked on photos which he says are perfect but which he does not always follow, adding or removing letters which do not correspond to the original. Moreover, he has discovered words which do not exist, either in Hebrew or Aramaic. In fine, he has left out one whole line and, to justify this procedure, has accused the engraver of the lamella of not having 'a hand used to writing'."

In a short article in *La Terra Santa*, [63] Testa returns to the subject and presents a list of all the letters in Milik's facsimile which do not correspond to the original. Illustrations are in the form of two photographs of the original and one each of Testa's and Milik's facsimiles. This permits even a reader less skilled in palaeography to make at least a material comparison between the letters in the two facsimiles and those in the photos of the original. The commentary accompanying the pictures helps us understand better those details where the naked eye and the photos (not too clear as to some finer points) can make a mistake.

Testa presented a fuller reply in *Biblica*. There he showed that the facsimile done by Milik strays in many details from the original. The result is a strange translation, and the more so, seeing that it is based on words which do not exist. Testa adds that Milik's translation does not run like that of amulets, neither with regard to the formulae used nor with regard to the object or person invoked as witness. In fact, there is no other amulet where one finds an exorcism made in the name of the Law, as Milik had claimed in his translation. Finally, according to Testa, the exorcisms end, not with

---

62   E. Testa, "Una Falsificazione della Laminella dell'Unzione," in *LTS* 44 (1968), 55-58.

best wishes for peace — *Šalom* — but with Amen. [64]

With regard to the dating, Testa observes that Milik took no account either of the fact that the lamella was found side by side with Herodian lamps, or of the palaeographic pictures at the beginning of his book. He adds: "Because they did not take into account the evidence of the Beduin and of possible palaeographic comparisons, there are cases of serious scholars doubting the chronology of well-known and safely-established documents, amongst them, those of Qumran." As can be guessed, Testa is referring to Zeitlin. In this instance Milik followed Zeitlin though he had written of the latter's stand, "at present it cannot be taken seriously any more." [65]

J. Starcky, in a review which appeared in the *Revue Biblique*, [66] shared Milik's views. However, he has never handled the lamella in question. On the other hand, reviews which note a reference to the sacrament of the anointing of the sick have recently been written, for example, by L.-M. Orrieux and A. Janssen. The former says, "The deep study done by Fr. Testa throws a new light on the sacrament of the sick as practised by the Catholic and the Orthodox Churches." [67] Janssen states, "Above all, it is what the inscription contains that is important. There it speaks, as we can put it, of the anointing of the sick." [68]

Daniélou also took an interest in the lamella and recognized Testa's work as "a new contribution to research on the Judaeo-Christians." [69] He writes, further, that "Testa's thesis can be debated

64 E. Testa, "Ancora sulla laminella giudeo-cristiana," in *Biblica* 49 (1968), 249-253.
65 J. T. Milik, *Dieci anni di scoperte nel deserto di Giuda*. Turin, 1957, 11.
66 J. Starcky, Review of *LHF* in *RB* 75 (1968), 278-280.
67 L.-M. Orrieux, in *Lumière et vie* 16 (1967), no. 85, 113-115. Subsequently, he was influenced by Milik: cfr. *Lumière et vie* 17 (1968), no. 86, 122.
68 A. Janssen, in *Ephemerides Theologicae Lovanienses* 43 (1967), 608.
69 Review in *Recherches de Science Religieuse* 56 (1968), 119-120.

both with regard to its sacramental significance and its Jewish Christian origin. However, he has supported it with solid arguments" which can be reduced to the matter of literary documentation and the use of symbols in other lamellae.

On December 14, 1968, Fr. Testa held a conference on the lamella in the "Casa Nova," Jerusalem, showing new and clearer photos. These we have used in the present publication. (figg. 27-28).

7. The manuscript of 'Abd el-Jabbar.

We have spoken of many discoveries relative to Jewish Christianity and of what has been published in connection with this subject. Far from representing a conclusion, all this is but a beginning in this new field of study. An abundance of literary and archaeological material is still hidden, either in archives or in the very earth itself. For this reason, scholars feel that they should tread lightly, sensing that they should go forward in this domain of investigation with great care, especially with regard to those places where, it is thought, the Judaeo-Christians lived on for a considerable time.

It was therefore with great satisfaction that all interested in the field of Jewish Christian studies welcomed the news (promptly spread by world-wide radio and press) that a tenth century manuscript had been found, authored by one 'Abd el-Jabbar who made use of a Jewish Christian document. The text was found in Istanbul, and shows likenesses with another which was known under the name of "The Gospel of Barnabas."

Professor Shlomo Pines dealt with it in a long article.[70] From the excerpts published, it is not always clear what is taken from

---

70 Sh. Pines, *The Jewish-Christians of the Early Centuries of Christianity according to a New Source.* Jerusalem, 1966. (Israel Academy of Sciences and Humanities, II, n. 13.)

the original document and what has been reedited by the Arab writer. This makes it harder to decide the date of the writing and what periods the document actually reflects. Pines suggests as the date the fourth-fifth centuries, but it would seem advisable to wait for the final publication of the document before assessing it at its full value. [71]

Meanwhile, as Daniélou remarks in a detailed review, [72] what we can state confidently is that the discovery of this work is in line with the data already established by the Fathers of "The Flagellation" regarding the presence of Judaeo-Christians, not only during the early centuries, but also in later times down to the fourth century. If I am not mistaken, the document is a reflection of the struggle which took place in Palestine during the Constantine period between the Judaeo-Christians and those of Gentile stock.

It is likely that the document provides new data for a study of the different tendencies which developed within Jewish Christianity itself. At the present time, we have to hand many details on the existence and form of the Jewish Christian Church. Naturally, we would like to be able to differentiate between the various currents of thought which certainly existed within that community and which gradually became more prominent. It is obvious that this work will take time and that it requires the collaboration of many scholars.

The manuscript in question is all the more important in that it presents an opportunity to study and to establish the first relationships between the Christian religion and Islam, as likewise the influence which Jewish Christianity exercised over Islam itself. According to Testa, who is still studying the question, it is already

---

71 Reservations are expressed by E. Bammel in *Novum Testamentum* 10 (1968), 1-9.

72 J. Daniélou, in *Recherches de Science Religieuse* 55 (1967), 96-99.

recognized that the Christianity known to Mohammed derived from Judaeo-Christians and that many teachings in the Qoran are to be traced back to the latter. Perhaps, if we take these relationships into account, we can the better understand the decisions — many contradictory — which are to be found in the Qoran with respect to Christians. Those of Gentile origin could hardly expect either that the first Moslems would be very sympathetic towards them or that the Christian name would stand very highly with the first Islamic writers.

The clay lamps discovered in Palestine, side by side with coins of the seventh and eighth centuries, tend to confirm what we have just said. With the arrival of Islam in Palestine, the Byzantines had to depart. Artists in the country felt free to embark on a new program using Eastern motifs. Technically, and especially from the viewpoint of iconography, this implied relationship with the Jewish Christian tradition which was already known from the ossuaries and other monuments with a funerary character. The new art-forms tended to stress the meaning of the Cross which had already been presented in manifold ways. [73] Later, when the Moslems became more powerful, taking control of the whole political situation, such representations became impossible and archaeology testifies that they gradually disappeared.

8. *The excavations at Capernaum.*

On the occasion of the nineteenth centenary of the death of St. Peter, the Custody of the Holy Land thought it right that the shrines dedicated to the chief apostle on the shore of the Lake of Tiberias should be refurbished. There was question of Tabgha, where

---

73 B. Bagatti, "Lucerne fittili di Palestina dei secoli VII-VIII," in *Rivista di Archeologia cristiana* 40 (1964), 253-269.

Christ conferred the primacy on Peter, and of Capernaum, where St. Peter had his home.

At Capernaum, as was expected, much new material came to light. From the outset, it was bound to have Jewish Christian associations, given the fact of its high antiquity, as also St. Peter's mission amongst the first Judaeo-Christians (Gal. 2:9).

In Capernaum, Jesus visited many homes, teaching and working wonders. There is mention of the houses of Matthew, Jairus, the Centurion, and Peter. However, so far as we know, it was only in Peter's home that veneration of Christ's presence lived on through the ages. A saying attributed to Aetheria has it that, "In Capernaum, however, the house of the chief of the apostles has been turned into a church, the walls of which are still standing, just as they were." [74] This means that, at that time, the house was still preserved, but changed into a place of worship.

Another text, written about 570 by the Piacenza Pilgrim, reads, "We came to Capernaum, to the home of Blessed Peter which today is a basilica." [75] At this time, the house had given way to a basilica, that is, a place of worship.

In view of these statements, it was greatly desired that excavations be undertaken to see whether they were to be believed or not. After what happened at Nazareth, there were hopes that something meaningful would be found.[76] A chance came when Fr. Virgilio Corbo, a noted Franciscan archaeologist, was charged with the task of examining the whole area containing memoirs of St. Peter's home. Straight after Easter, on Tuesday, April 16, 1968,

74 D. Baldi, *Enchiridion Locorum Sanctorum.* Jerusalem, 1955, no. 443, p. 299.
75 *Idem,* no. 436, p. 297.
76 P. Andrès, "La casa di S. Pietro a Cafarnao," in *LTS* 39 (1963), 54-58; B. Bagatti, *L'Eglise de la gentilité en Palestine.* Jerusalem, 1968, 199-200. For inaccurate news spread in 1967, see *LTS* 44 (1968), 296-298.

he set to work. For a start, he had to dig trenches to get some idea of the levels. At the end, Fr. Corbo discovered the partial remains of the home of St. Peter just as they stood before the building of the eight-sided Byzantine church began.

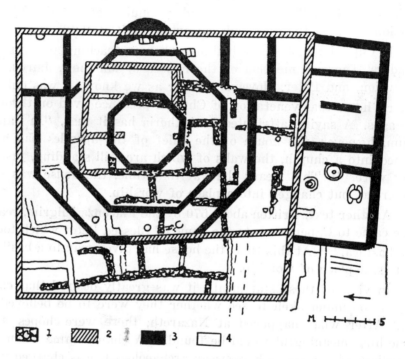

Fig. 29. Plan of the House of St. Peter in Capernaum (from *Guida di Cafarnao*, p. 48).

The mosaic flooring and the octagonal plan relate the Byzantine structure to those in use in the fifth-sixth centuries. This dating is confirmed by the discovery of coins of the same period. One was found within the apse, in the limestone plaster of the baptismal pool, built at the same time as the church. Another was discovered lower down in older surroundings, covered with refuse which had been used as a fill when the floor of the building was raised one metre higher.

Amongst the debris, and in the earth itself, remains of pottery dating back to the first-fifth centuries were found. Amidst the stones, several metres of plaster with decorative designs were brought to light, as likewise traces of ornamented walls. Various motifs can be deciphered from the wash: different colored stripes,

Fig. 30. Graffito in Greek in the Jewish Christian Church
of Capernaum (from *LA* XVIII, p. 51).

geometrical shapes, flowers and fruit. Many graffiti, evidence that the place was frequented by pilgrims, were discovered. Actually, several pieces of plaster show scratchings and scribblings. Sometimes these were rough in form, sometimes finely executed. Letters and phrases in Greek, Hebrew and Syriac have been deciphered. Thus, we have archaeological documentation of a Jewish Christian church similar to that at Nazareth. In fact, the Hebrew inscriptions can only derive from Jewish Christian circles. A graffito with a prayer to Christ was found intact and this shows, beyond all doubt, the Christian nature of the place. (Cfr. Plate 15.)

At the end of the first campaign of digging, we can already follow the successive periods of worship here, from the first to about the fifth-sixth centuries: originally in *the house* itself, roughly decorated and rich in graffiti, then in the improvised synagogue and, fiinally, in the Byzantine basilica.

From the time of the first finds, the excavation attracted the attention of many scholars and experts on Palestiniana. Fr. Corbo has given a preliminary report of the first two campaigns and will provide much more detail later.[77]

77 V. Corbo, "La casa del Principe degli Apostoli ritrovata a Cafarnao," in *L'Osservatore Romano*, June 29-30, 1968, p. 8. Scientific report in *LA* 18 (1968), 5-54. Translated by S. Saller: *The House of St. Peter at Capharnaum*. Jerusalem, 1969. More popular description, translated by G. Bushell: *New Memoirs of Saint Peter by the Sea of Galilee*. Jerusalem, 1969.

CHAPTER III

THE PUBLICATIONS

The abundance of Jewish-Christian data found in various places, and made up of many diverse objects, already permits scholars to take an overall, comprehensive view. It has made possible closer comparisons and still more accurate interpretations. Thanks to the work of archaeological and literary investigators, the whole ground is now much more solid. In the beginning, the symbols on ossuaries and other monuments seemed very strange. Now they have been given their proper meaning.

The Church of the Circumcision has been studied and analyzed with respect to its history and its theological ideas. It has been placed in its appropriate framework. Monographs on many Jewish Christian subjects have been published, giving a fuller knowledge of the detail. All this has been made possible by a deeper re-examination of the abundant material brought to light.

1. *General résumé of the finds*

In 1957, a new professor for the Franciscan House of Biblical Studies, at "The Flagellation," arrived in Jerusalem: Fr. Emmanuel Testa. He had followed the courses of Professor Eugenio Zolli, former Grand Rabbi of Rome. It is no exaggeration to say that, with Fr. Testa's coming to Jerusalem, the study of Christian Antiquities in the Holy Land took a new turn. On the bases of ancient and modern literature on the subject, research on Jewish Christianity was broadened and more fully illustrated, especially from the theological angle. Study of epigraphical and archaeological material was taken up and extended to ossuaries and all other objects to hand.

The ossuaries discovered at "Dominus Flevit" more than one hundred years ago had been carefully washed and cleaned up by Brother Michelangelo Tizzani, the alert custodian of the shrine. While tidying up the various items, he found symbols which were unknown to scholars who had been interested in the subject. Some of these signs were traced on the upper edge of ossuaries, others on the lower. Some were inside, covered by the human remains which had been laid there. All this was new material which, to the layman, was perhaps unimportant, but which, for the experts concerned with the study, gave ground for challenging at least one archaeologist's theory that the marks simply served to show where the lid should be fitted.

In the meantime, the archaeologists Bagatti and Testa made the rounds of ossuary collections looking for symbols hitherto unedited. Besides those kept in the Museum of "The Flagellation," the two experts studied those in the Museum of the Department of Antiquities and in the Palestine Museum, those in the Dominican Fathers' and the White Fathers' collections, those kept at Bezalel and those in the garden of Dr. Joseph Free's school on Mount Olivet. The material viewed and studied was quite abundant. Some hundreds of ossuaries were involved. The two scholars made copies and photos of the inscriptions and symbols they bore.

The letters most often encountered were *alpha, omicron, aleph,* X and *taw.* Amongst the symbols, there recurred the star, the plough and the "cosmic ladder." Testa set himself to the task of interpreting such signs. He looked for a key in a study of the literature contemporary with the archaeological finds. After some time, he succeeded in discovering many texts pertaining to the Jewish Christian Church of the period. These gave meaning to the symbols traced on ossuaries and on the walls of burial chambers.

Thus, for instance, the *Apocalypse* helped explain very well the apocalyptic letters of the alphabet used in relation to Christ. Hermas' *Shepherd* gave a clue to the sixpointed star. The *Odes of Solomon* threw light on flower designs.

Once the symbols were classified and brought into relationship with those already known and firmly interpreted, two questions remained to be solved : first and before all, did the ossuaries date back before or after the time of Christ; secondly, were the people using the ossuaries amongst "those who had given their names to Christ" or had they remained faithful to the synagogue?

The Franciscan scholars endeavoured to answer both questions. Bagatti listed all known ossuaries and sought to date not only the various objects found in the same excavations but, above all, the pottery found inside the ossuaries themselves. Through this examination he reached the conclusion that, contrary to what some experts had stated, there was nothing to prove that the ossuaries went back to pre-Christian times. In fact, it was necessary to distinguish the ossuaries from the burial chambers for the latter were certainly older and did not originally contain the ossuaries which were deposited therein in later times.

This problem was being studied simultaneously by the Israel Department of Antiquities and, substantially, the same conclusions were reached by both sides. In fact, L.Y. Rahmani noted that the theory of those who would date the ossuaries found in the burial chambers at Gezer back in the Maccabean period is untenable, and this in view of the fact that all other objects found there are no earlier than the Herodian lamps discovered in the same place.[1]

---

1   L. Y. Rahmani, in *'Atiqot* 3 (1961), 116-117.

The custom of exhuming.

With regard to the second question concerning those who used the ossuaries (a practice which presupposes exhumation), Testa made a careful study of all the Talmudic literature relative to this custom. The result was that he did not find one passage favoring the usage. Exhumation was allowed only in certain well-defined cases as, for example, when the deceased had not been buried in the family tomb. He stressed that the few Talmudic texts which had been quoted by experts against the Christian character of the ossuaries had reference to the burial of bones rediscovered *outside* cemeteries, in public places (roads, squares, etc.) or in common graves (in the case of criminals). The object of reburial was that they "would be reunited in peace with their fathers."

Testa remained convinced that the Jews always, in former times as at present, have had a horror of touching human bones because of the legal impurity involved. This was one reason why experts like Levy and Chwolson had rejected the theory of Clermont-Ganneau. From the outset, the latter had stated that the little stone boxes found in tombs, the so-called "ossuaries," or, later, "osteo-thekes," were not meant to hold treasures (as Saulcy had held) but simply the bones of the dead. The difficulty raised against Clermont-Ganneau was always the same, namely, Hebrew Law forbidding contact with the remains of the dead.[2]

An analytic study of proper names is very important in trying to determine the religious faith of those buried in ossuaries. Testa undertook the work and transcribed all the names found on the hundreds of ossuaries examined. The result is that, of the 218 names found, 62 are of Old Testament origin, common to both Christians and Jews; 62 are from the New Testament and rare amongst Jews; 91 were in common use during the first three centuries and amongst

2   Cfr. *RB* 9 (1900), 109 and 308.

people of both faiths. Only ten names are proper to those found in rabbinic circles of Palestine. From this, Testa concludes that, even by reason of this connection through the proper names, we can say that the ossuaries are to be ascribed to Christians rather than to Jews.

Meaning of the term "proselyte."

It need hardly be added that, with a view to deciding archaeological problems, inscriptions are of the utmost importance. Now, amongst the inscriptions found at "Dominus Flevit," there was one (no. 21) which read, "Jude, proselyte." It was found in the same ossuary which bore the "Constantine monogram." In his review of Bagatti's book, de Vaux went against the opinion of the author saying, "Until the contrary is proven, this proselyte is a Jew, like the proselyte Diogenes of ossuary no. 81, and the proselyte Salome of ossuary no. 97." [3]

Avi-Yonah, in his review of the same work, does well to make a distinction amongst the various names which are followed by the term "proselyte." In this connection, he writes, "The case of ossuary no. 21 is especially complex because the person buried therein is called (according to the lettering of Milik), 'Jude, son of Jude, the proselyte.' The ossuary is marked with a *Chi-Rho*. It is clear that a person whose father was named Jude could not be a convert to Judaism. On the other hand, in Greek the adjective 'proselyte' is used exclusively of converts to Judaism. Do we have to suppose that a Gentile proselyte (a) had changed his name ; (b) had changed that of his father ; (c) had subsequently passed over from Judaism to Christianity ? Stranger things have happened but let us produce more solid arguments to prove them." [4]

---

3   R. De Vaux, in *RB* 66 (1959), 300.
4   M. Avi-Yonah, in *Israel Exploration Journal* 11 (1961), 94.

We think that Avi-Yonah replies adequately to de Vaux who, as we have said, interpreted the term "proselyte" in a Jewish sense. In other words, Avi-Yonah means that the Jude in question cannot be a proselyte to Judaism seeing that his name already identifies him as of Jewish origin.

For this reason, Testa returned to the subject.[5] He used ancient texts to prove that the word "proselyte" was in use amongst Judaeo-Christians, and was applied by them to all who came over to Christianity from any other religion whatsoever, the Jewish included. Thus, the word which had formed a difficulty for de Vaux turned out to be the key whereby the Christian character of the ossuaries was established.

The purpose of exhumation.

Another problem concerning the ossuaries is to fix the purpose of exhumation. Why disinter the mortal remains of the dead to place them in ossuaries ? Some archaeologists held that this was done for purely practical purposes, something like what is in mind at the present time, namely, to save space and prevent cemeteries from spreading too far. After a full study of the problem, the Israeli scholar, Rahmani, wrote: "We have already suggested elsewhere that the custom of gathering bones in ossuaries destined for one person, or for individuals closely related, corresponds to the concept of the resurrection of the dead which was current amongst the Pharisees in opposition to the Sadducees. Evidently, the presence of many remains in ossuaries is a sign of the large use made of them. In the very tombs of Sanhedria, there are many *kokhim* and there cannot be simply question of a desire to economize. The same family which was sufficiently affluent to have 80 *kokhim* dug in the rocky walls of their tomb could have easily afforded the luxury

---

5   E. Testa, *ISGC*, 114; also in *LTS* 39 (1963), 132-138.

of increasing the number of *kokhim* or of adding another room to the grave. If, however, the bones were brought together in special ossuaries, and not in the common ones, we have to look for a reason elsewhere." [6]

An assessment of all the arguments in favour of the Christian character of the ossuaries implies consideration of: the Jewish prohibition about touching the bones of the dead, the use of ossuaries with the resurrection in view, the observance of this custom by Christians in later periods, the lack of absolute arguments in favour of this practice amongst Christians of the first period, the presence of data which cannot be explained otherwise, the Christian nature of most of the names and, finally, the descriptions which follow some names engraved on the ossuaries. None of these elements are met with in the tombs of the large (Jewish) cemetery at Bet Še'arim. There, the remains of Jews who, for the most part, had come to Galilee after the Second Jewish War, were brought together and buried. Therefore, Testa concludes that *all* the ossuaries are to be ascribed to Judaeo-Christians.

Rahmani had hinted that the sect of the Pharisees might have made use of ossuaries but Testa observes that the texts forbidding the exhuming of the dead (with a view to placing them in ossuaries) have their origin precisely amongst the descendants of the Pharisee sect. Flagrant violation on the scale indicated by the large number of ossuaries found would surely not have been tolerated.

Concurrence of Fr. Daniélou.

It would not be fair to pass over the fact that Frs. Bagatti and Testa realized the value of their discoveries thanks largely to a book written by Fr. Daniélou.[7] It is not our task to elaborate on this

6   L.Y. Rahmani, in *'Atiqot* 3 (1961), 117.
7   J. Daniélou, *Théologie du Judéo-Christianisme*. Paris, 1958.

work, seeing that it does not enter our field directly. However, it saved hours of literary research for the Franciscan scholars. It also provided a theological basis for the comprehension and fresh interpretation of all the finds previously made. It contains the following noteworthy themes : the study of the sources; the delineation of the Jewish Christian sect; study of the exegesis and apocalyptic ideas of the Jewish Christian Church; a long and detailed treatment of Jewish Christian teaching; ideas on the Trinity and the angels; a study of the titles reserved for the Son of God; the doctrines of the Incarnation, Redemption and the Mystery of the Cross ; ideas on Millenarianism, Christian initiation and baptismal rites.

I have in hand the copy of Daniélou's book, *Theologie du Judéo-Christianisme,* from Fr. Testa's own private library. I must say how greatly impressed I have been to see how deeply he has studied this work. Everywhere, there are notes, references, words underscored, additions, small sketches — all evidence of how patiently Testa worked to bring the Jewish Christian symbolism studied by him into relationship with the first Christian theology, traced through the ancient writers like Papias, Irenaeus and Clement of Alexandria and back again to the time of the apostles themselves. For us who are accustomed to Hellenistic formulation, the whole might seem to be something quite foreign to our familiar rule of faith.

The symbolism of the Judaeo-Christians.

On January 18, 1961, in the Aula Magna of the Pontifical Biblical Institute, Rome, Fr. Testa expounded the results of his long research on the symbolism of the Judaeo-Christians. His dissertation for the degree of Doctor in Sacred Scripture was approved, with the commendation "summa cum laude." [8] The conclusions of the thesis had already been announced by Fr. Bagatti in an article

8   Cfr. *Biblica* 42 (1961), 491.

which filled the whole of page 4 in *L'Osservatore Romano*. [9] This was afterwards reprinted in *La Terra Santa*.

From the article, Daniélou got news about the signs which his studies of the ancient literature had led him to believe must have existed somewhere. He therefore decided to gather together some of his previous publications on the subject and to illustrate them by means of the new archaeological discoveries in Jerusalem. Thus, for the very first time, there appeared the archaeological documentation of the meaning of the cross under the axe, the six-pointed star, the Christ-Angel, the plough as a symbol of Christ, and so on. [10] As a result, the publication of the full material brought together and studied by Testa himself was all the more eagerly awaited. It was printed in the first months of 1962, a handsome and copiously illustrated book. [11]

Contents of the book.

We think it useful to present a résumé of the rich contents of this work, though we have already hinted at them here and there already. Thus, the reader can get some idea of the whole at one glance.

In the preface, the author speaks of the debate between the "Realists" and the "Symbolists," in so far as the signs are concerned, relative to the letters and the numbers often found on the ancient Christian monuments. He explains the principles at issue and makes a criticism of them. He then presents those principles which will

9 B. Bagatti, "Una pagina inedita della Chiesa primitiva," in *L'Osservatore Romano*, August 6, 1960; also in *LTS* 36 (1960), 230-236.

10 J. Daniélou, *Les symboles chrétiens primitifs.* Paris, 1961, See also P. Ternant in *Proche-Orient Chrétien* 13 (1963), 344-345.

11 E. Testa, *Il simbolismo dei Giudeo-cristiani.* Jerusalem, 1962. Pp. xxxii-590, with 47 Plates. (Publications of the Franciscan House of Biblical Studies, no. 14.)

guide him in the exposition and explanation of the symbolism of the Judaeo-Christians.

As chapter I shows, those principles can be broken down to: (a) The sacred language expressed by mystic letters and words (e. g. Alpha and Omega) together with sacred tongues governed by the *notarikon*, an exegesis already known to the rabbis and classical writers; (b) the sacred numbers which have a symbolic and theological, rather than a mathematical significance (e. g. 1000 means a period of prosperity) — these governed by the *gematria* and the *isopsēphia* by which one or more names correspond to the numbers which are yielded by their letters taken as numbers (e. g. 666 is Antichrist; 888 is Jesus); (c) the seals which consist of designs (plough, tree, etc.) and of symbols to be used on "initiates" to show their membership in a more or less esoteric group; (d) the "sacred names" which were those of God and Christ believed to be full of force in themselves and the more so when expressed in monograms; (e) "the hidden mystery" which consisted in concealing the foregoing mystic symbols, thus stressing the mystical and esoteric value of the symbolism itself.

In chapter II, the author shows that these five elements are found to be brought together in the ancient Christian documents. He quotes some taken from the inspired sources (e. g. the Apocalypse), from Judaizing sources (e. g. the Aleppo lamella), from Gnostic backgrounds, from the "mystic words" of Pacomius and from the Khirbet Kilkish steles.

After demonstrating the existence of a symbolic system, expressed in literary and archaeological documents, the author goes on to list in his next chapter (III) the symbols found in the "Dominus Flevit" excavations. These form the archaeological basis for the whole book. Testa examines the question as to whether they belong in the domain of symbolism itself. He discounts the idea that they are merely casual or practical signs.

In the following chapters, he shows that the "Dominus Flevit" signs are undoubtedly symbolic. In chapter IV he studies the signs which take the form of letters and shows, by means of first century texts, that they belong to Jewish Christian doctrine. In chapter V he does the same relative to number-signs, and then reconstructs the whole system of sacred arithmetic in use in the primitive Church. He lays special stress on the fact that this arithmetic had meaning particularly with reference to the dead and speaks of the "dyptichs" and "platonics." In line with these he describes the lists of names and numbers found on two covers of the Bethphage ossuaries.

In the longest and richest chapter, on Jewish Christian theology (ch. VI), the author aims to show that the "Dominus Flevit" signs in monogrammatic form are nothing else but signs of the cross.

He takes as his literary basis hymn XIX of Paulinus of Nola, on the artistic drawings of the cross, together with the famous text of St. Justin. He divides the material into Trinitarian signs (symbolized by the triangle); dynamic signs (the *waw* cross, the cross with horns: two, three or six), thus developing the Jewish Christian teaching on the angels as outward manifestations of the power of the Trinity; prophetic signs, leading on to the theory that deeds and sayings in the Old Testament are prophetic signs of the cross of Christ, e. g. the Ark of Noah, Jacob's ladder, the bloodstained lintels of Jewish homes, the serpent of Moses, the star of Jacob, the tree of life; cosmic signs implying the universality of salvation expressed in the square cross and the cross in the globe. Lastly, he deals with the saving fruits of the cross expressed in such symbols as the plough, the 'Anḥ-cross (or Egyptian symbol of life), the Ḥamt-cross (symbol of the womb), the axe-cross, the fecund cross (bound up with Millenarianism), with which latter the grave of Nur, in the third century, found at Bethphage, must be associated.

In ch. VII the author proves that the monogram signs of "Dominus Flevit" refer to the name of Jesus, as also some letter-seals (e. g. *A*, *T*, etc.). He shows how some monogram forms (like *IH*) and the theological type of the "rock" refer to the typology of Joshua in the Old Testament. Other monograms (like *Rho* and the *chrismon*) are related to the "centenarian" Abraham, father of the miraculous "Son of Promise." The so-called monogram of Constantine is an ancient sign, bound up with the number for Jesus, 888, and the title "Soter" is tied up with the number 5. Lastly, he deals with mnemonic substitutions for Christ, the Dove (which as Alpha-Omega corresponds to the number 801) and the Fish (which answers to the number of empire, 27). Thus, the author ends his proof that the "signs" of "Dominus Flevit" are symbolic.

These signs could not have formed part of the well-known Jewish system of symbols, for that of the Judaeo-Christians was incompatible with it. This is shown in chapter VIII. For this precise reason *all* of the ossuaries, rich in such symbols of the latter folk, just cannot be Jewish. An additional reason for this conclusion is the rabbinical teaching on the impurity of bones which, for Christians, on the other hand, were something sacred. Underlying this Christian concept is the doctrine of the Mystical Body and the practice of venerating relics.

Because of all this, the ossuaries cannot be ascribed to Maccabean times. All date from the first to the second century, A. D. The inscriptions, with the titles and names, confirm this theory since they are derived from the New Testament. No reason to deny this is found in the title "proselyte," seeing that it was given by the Judaeo-Christians even to Jews who wished to become Christians.

In chapter IX the author aims to show that the Jewish Christian symbolism and the Church of the Circumcision were known both to the rabbis of the second to the fourth century (there is evidence of many debates between followers of the two systems and faiths) and to the Fathers of the Great Church, especially Irenaeus, Justin, Origen and Cyril. In the fourth century, disputes were still continuing, as is evident from the works of Gregory of Nyssa, Chrysostom, John II and Rufinus. Jerome and Epiphanius, on the other hand, are at least partially favourable to such symbolism. Different

Church Councils, from the fourth century on, were to oppose the system seeing that it had often degenerated into superstition. Nevertheless, the symbol remained in use especially amongst the mystics, the common people and particularly amongst the Copts.

Besides this general plan, Testa's book is enriched with seven *Excursus* or special essays dealing with : the symbolism of the heterodox; the "elements" of this world ; the laws of the sacred arithmetic; the cross as a "good sign"; the powers of the name of Jesus; the Church and her constitution; the initiation of the Judaeo-Christians. In addition, there is a detailed bibliography and a large analytical index relative to the symbols.

Bagatti wrote a historical introduction. He makes it clear that the Judaeo-Christians did not go out of existence in 135 A.D. but continued on within the Church until the end of the sixth century. Besides, he supplied some archaeological notes, particularly on the chronology of the ossuaries.

Needless to say, some of Testa's statements and conclusions have overthrown many ideas which were taken for granted up till the present. Other views which had been held only provisionally were confirmed. To do all this, he had to re-study much material already published, such as some funerary lamellae and, in particular, the Aleppo lamella now kept in the Museum of "The Flagellation." He had to examine the finds at Nazareth, especially a pool bearing signs and graffiti which reproduce letters and symbols from the time of the first building there. He also made use of some thirty marked stones deriving from Khirbet Kilkish.

Opinions and approval of the experts.

L. Moraldi had the good fortune to spend a year in Palestine and thus was able to follow closely the research on the symbolism of the Judaeo-Christians done by Testa. He was responsible for a detailed description of it in *Rivista Biblica* : "It is a pioneer work on a subject which, today as previously, does not meet with the sympathy of many. For all, it is somewhat burdensome because of its particular limitations which have not always been respected. Testa has avoided these difficulties.... Most impressive is the scientific apparatus, the patient and prudent gathering and elaboration of material which have allowed important conclusions to be drawn and which can be taken as already proven. Amongst the signs found on the ossuaries of 'Dominus Flevit', those found around Jerusalem, on the walls at Nazareth and on the steles of Khirbet Kilkish, there are symbols which are certainly to be ascribed to the Judaeo-Christians of Palestine. It is now evident that the hitherto commonly held idea that no trace of such people remained in Jerusalem after 135 is devoid of foundation. There is no doubt that research on the history and theology of the Judaeo-Christians is still full of surprises." [12]

Fr. G. Rinaldi was also in touch with the finds by reason of his visit to the Middle East. He writes : "Perhaps, the interpretations could be better defined, arranged and graded. Some witnesses may be judged superfluous, others (and here we think of the liturgy) could have been added. However, it is unmistakeable that the thesis presented is not only the outcome of the writer's work; it lies in the very facts he presents. It is quite surprising that, with such an abundance of data, the problem was not treated long before. But, this only serves to stress the great difference between the ways of expression in the Jewish Christian world, two thousand years ago, and those to which we are accustomed." [13]

A work of this kind could not escape the attention of Daniélou. He reviewed it with special care.[14] First, he stated that the new

---

12 L. Moraldi, "Nuova luce sui giudeo-cristiani in un libro recente," in *Rivista Biblica* 11 (1963), 196-205.
13 G. Rinaldi, in *Bibbia e Oriente* 5 (1963), 79-80.
14 J. Daniélou, in *Recherches de Science Religieuse* 51 (1963), 117-121.

discoveries have given us a new knowledge of primitive Jewish Christianity. He goes on to speak of the contribution made by the Franciscan House of Biblical Studies of "The Flagellation." He plainly states that some scholars had debated the Christian character of the new finds. Then he adds : "The arguments brought forward by Frs. Testa and Bagatti are, for the most part, quite convincing. Moreover, many symbols and signs are found on monuments which are specifically Christian." Seeing that Jews were strictly forbidden to touch corpses, the very existence of ossuaries is, for Daniélou, one of the most convincing arguments. He also stresses the fact that Testa in his work has always looked for support in literary sources. In fine, for Daniélou, there is question of definitive conclusions. "Testa's thesis is therefore solidly based. His book is, at the same time, a repertory in which the various kinds of Jewish Christian forms of symbolism are studied."

Having analysed different symbols he ends : "This book contributes generously to our knowledge of Jewish Christianity." After reviewing other works, Daniélou returns many times to Testa's conclusions with approval.[15]

In an article, Thomas Federici [16] sums up the present state of Jewish Christian studies. He is careful to stress that the archaeological finds in Palestine relative to this subject should not be regarded as "lucky." They are the result of patient study and research. According to him *Il simbolismo* by Testa is an inexhaustible mine of information on pertinent data, with appropriate analysis and synthesis. For studies on Jewish Christianity the book is a monumental work. Federici adds that Testa "interprets many things with surety, other he leaves ... to those who will come after, noting

---

15   J. Daniélou, in *Mullus*. Münster, 1964, 50.

16   T. Federici, "Il simbolismo dei Giudeo-cristiani," in *L'Osservatore Romano*, January 21, 1965; also, in *LTS* 41 (1965), 46-50.

the problems involved. Even the inevitable critics, some few of whom appeared at first, showing scant knowledge of the subject, will agree with others that a book like this means that a decisive stage has been reached in research in one particular sector and that it will give rise straightway to other fruitful investigations." [17]

Fr. Evode Beaucamp, reviewing the book,[18] notes the particular importance of the finds relative to the Judaeo-Christians which seem to throw new light on certain currents of thought already suggested by the discovery of the library at Qumran. He stresses the immediacy of the problem and adds that, all things considered, the book gives the impression that we are on solid ground. The clear conclusions presented by Testa compensate for the fatigue the reader will sometimes feel as he perseveres with the reading of the book. Beaucamp states that the composition of such a volume must have cost the author an immense amount of work. However, this is rewarded by the result since the work will stand for many a day as the basic source for all students of Jewish Christianity. Besides being of interest for the exegesis of the New Testament and the study of Church history, the volume has something to offer students of the Coptic tradition and also of Islam. The reason for the latter is that the heterodox sects must have had an influence — still not too clearly defined — on the formation of the Qoran and the first Moslem traditions.

Fr. A. Aldama, S. J.[19] reviews the book from the viewpoint of Patristics. The work offers a contribution towards our better understanding of texts which refer to Jewish Christianity. These are now seen to throw new light on primitive Christian literature. *Il simbolismo* opens up vast horizons. "To quote but one example, the various

17   Idem, in *LTS* 41 (1965), 50.
18   E. Beaucamp, in *LA* 12 (1961-1962), 334-338.
19   J. A. De Aldama, in *Estúdios Eclesiásticos* 41 (1966), 579-580.

forms of the cross found at 'Dominus Flevit' clearly illustrate the verses of Paulinus of Nola's poem XIX." The reviewer ends by saying that the book deserves the attention of scholars and offers points of view which are interesting for the study of Patristics.

From the viewpoint of patrology still, the volume "Simbolismo" has been used by Fr. Raniero Cantalamessa, O.F.M. Cap. in his commentary on the homily "On Easter," sometimes attributed to St. Hyppolitus [19a]. He states that the book is "particularly interesting for archaeological evidence." From "Simbolismo" he takes two illustrations of the *Cheroma* and the *Pleroma*. The author would like to have a date relative to the two examples, but Fr. Testa after stating that they are to be found on ossuaries studied by him, takes it for granted that his treatment of the subject has been studied. There, he deals extensively with the question of the date and fixes it in the first or second century A.D.

Angelo Penna reviewed our work in its Italian edition [19b]. He suggests that we should await further studies in order to be able to judge the Jewish Christian movement better. However, he reports something from his own personal experience when he writes, "We need to be very careful before quoting a text of St. Jerome's (which speaks of a particular interpretation or an opinion of the *Hebraei* or of the *Judaei* (or, rather, *Judaizantes*) as proof of a Jewish Christian theology or with a view to documenting some historic event. However, it remains a fact that, even with a very cursory knowledge of symbolism and other Jewish Christian elements, unforeseen horizons are revealed by a re-reading of the Letter to Paul (= *Epist.* 30), of the Pacomian texts translated by the Saint into Latin, and many other writings by this Father."

19a R. Cantalamessa, *L'Omilia "In S. Pascha" dello Pseudo Ippolito*. Ricerche sulla teologia dell'Asia Minore nella seconda metà del II secolo. Milano, 1967. Pp. 124-130.
19b In *Rivista Biblica* XVII (1969) 328.

Actually, as a young man, the reviewer had done close study on the Saint and he can therefore personally appreciate what new contributions have been made by research on the Judaeo-Christians.

Study of the Judaeo-Christians has also thrown new light on the history of the Church. In 1966, Fr. Carlo Martini, S.J., present Rector of the Pontifical Biblical Institute, Rome, gave a conference during the Nineteenth Bible Week. He analyzed Codex D of the *Acts of the Apostles* with a view to sketching the personality of St. Peter. Dealing with the additions peculiar to this document, he stated that they derive from an environment where the guidance of St. Luke was followed. In conclusion he said, "If light is thrown on this background as a result of study of language and style, as also of archaeology and history, it will be possible to have a better grasp not only of a curious phenomenon of textual history but also of an environment and mentality which form an important aspect of the Christianity of early times." Relative to archaeological discoveries he states expressly, "In particular, one should note the studies which will be dealt with by E. Testa during the proceeding of this same Bible Week under the title, 'Saint Peter in the thought of the Judaeo-Christians.'" [19c]

Morton Smith,[20] speaking of the work of Goodenough on Jewish symbolism, writes : that the interpretation of the latter on the value of simple signs is strongly supported by the material published by Testa. In this same connection (the explanation of symbolism), the book is also cited by N. Sēd [21] and Avi-Yonah. [22]

19c C. M. Martini, *La figura di Pietro secondo le varianti del Codice D negli Atti degli Apostoli*, in *S. Pietro. Atti della XIX Settimana biblica*. Brescia, 1967, p. 289.

20 M. Smith, in *Journal of Biblical Literature* 86 (1967), 56.

21 N. Séd, "Hymnes sur le Paradis de Saint-Ephrem et les traditions juives," in *Le Muséon LXXXI* (1968), 492, regarding no. 888.

22 M. Avi-Yonah (in collaboration with M. W. Prausnitz and D. Barag), *Excavations at Shavei Zion*. Rome, 1967. Cfr. p. 49 for the monogram cross, and p. 55 for the cross as tree of life.

The Benedictine, J. Meysing [23] considers the particular aspect of symbolism as based on numbers. He sees in the material gathered by Testa a complement to the development of such signs in a more recent period from their beginnings. Their interpretation is changed because it is applied to Christ. In other words, while the signs remain the same and identical in origin, their meaning was altered when used by Judaeo-Christians because the symbols became Christological.

G. Lomiento examined the book carefully to trace the main lines of procedure. He says: "We are not going into an assessment of the deciphering of the signs, since that is an epigraphical question. We intend to follow the author as he reconstructs Jewish Christian theology and its background. Moreover, that is the aim of the book, as indicated at the beginning. Ending his heavy task, the author is fully aware that he has given new orientations, not definitive solutions. He has sought to open up new horizons for the Christian archaeologist (who studies the value of the symbols on the monuments) and for the philologists and liturgists (who provide literary documentation). It is from this latter point of view that we intend to examine the work." [24] What he finds to be chiefly developed and quite fundamental is the sign of the cross in its various combinations.

Any Jewish scholar in contact with Testa's book will have reason to feel proud, for he will see much material from the heritage of his own culture illustrated. However, we are sure that this pride and satisfaction will be tinged with a certain feeling of disillusion, for everything is given meaning by that "sect" which was Christianity. In a word, Jewish scholars will find that, in the perspectives opened up by Testa, the orthodoxy of many monuments

23 J. Meysing, in *Revue de Sciences Religieuses* 39 (1965), 219-223.
24 G. Lomiento, in *Vetera Christianorum* 1 (1964), 168.

will disappear, and they will be seen to belong only in a qualified sense to the common culture. Accepting his conclusions, based on second century Hebrew texts, we must explain them in the light of Christ.

We can appreciate the well-known sensitiveness of Jewish scholars on this point, especially at present when all the energies of the people, including those which we call cultural, are being combined to reconstitute the nation of Israel. In some details, Testa has brought more precision to statements made by authors belonging to Israeli activist movements. Nevertheless, seven years after the publication of the book, his conclusions have not caused any kind of contrary reaction. If there has been any sort of response, it has been favourable. In fact, we find *Il simbolismo* included in the "Selected Bibliography" of *'Atiqot*, the official bulletin of the Department of Antiquities.[25]

The Jewish writer, M. Tagliacozzo[26] presents Fr. Testa's book, together with that by Fr. Bagatti, to his coreligionists with this introduction: "The field of Jewish historiography has been notably enlarged this century. Particulary since the World War, an ever-increasing band of scholars has undertaken work in this area of research. On the basis of new archaeological finds and unedited, rare documents, they aim to reconstruct the way of life and the changing fortunes known to the people of Palestine in the first centuries of our era. Amongst the non-Jewish scholars who have been busy with this kind of research, Fr. Emmanuel Testa of the Franciscan House of Biblical Studies in Jerusalem occupies a notable place because of his investigative work regarding the Judaeo-Christians." He then goes on to examine both books under the various headings. Of interest to us are the many technical Hebrew terms he encounters

---

25 *'Atiqot. Supplement to Vol.* 4, p. 4.
26 In *La Rassegna mensile di Israele* 34 (1968), 297-299.

when describing the different sections in the books dealing with both literature and monuments.

As we have noted, T. Federici speaks of critics who "show scant knowledge of the subject."[27] No names are mentioned but we know what he is hinting at. We think of Margherita Guarducci. In an article with the characteristic sub-title "Polemiche, chiarimenti, giudizi, " she examines *Il simbolismo*.[28] Many of the observations she makes are quite extraneous to the subject. Amongst others of a more scientific nature, she calls Fr. Testa to task for using v instead of f in his interpretation of *waw*. In the same article, several other scholars are in her sights: A. Ferrua, J.M.C. Toynbell, O. Cullmann, M. Maccarone, L. von Herlting, P.M. Fraser, P. Braun and J. Carcopino. Federici's reference might also call to mind the study by E. Dinkler,[29] a studious enough production, if you will, but cramped by a narrow outlook on Graeco-Roman culture. In fact, Dinkler's writing shows that he has not only failed to penetrate the Jewish Christian mentality but also that, in the example he mentions (on the interpretation of the mosaic in St. Mary Major's) he has misunderstood Testa. One can credit that *Il simbolismo* is not bread for every mouth, nor is it food that is readily digestible. Surely, it will not be purely negative reactions which will stimulate new research but those of specialists who foresee new insights and offer practical suggestions. It is on the work of the latter that fresh, scholary research is based and makes progress.

The Sacred Congregation for Religious Universities and Seminaries judged *Il simbolismo* a model of scientific research along the lines laid down by the Church. In this regard, Cardinal Pizzardo

27 T. Federici, in *LTS* 41 (1965), 50.
28 M. Guarducci, appendix to the article "Il fenomeno orientale del simbolismo alfabetico e i suoi sviluppi nel mondo cristiano d'Occidente." Offprint n. 62 of the Accademia dei Lincei. Rome, 1964, 487-490.
29 E. Dinkler, in *Jahrbuch für Antike und Christentum* 5 (1962), 108-109.

126

writes: "The group of scholars who are working so well at the
House of 'The Flagellation' is giving proof of how church science
can be made to progress, especially in the biblical field, without
impairing those principles which, in the past, have always guided
those who have merited well by enlightening the holy Church of God
through science." [30]

3. The Church of the Circumcision.

In his review of Testa's *Il simbolismo*, L. Moraldi had written:
"Bagatti cooperated in the work by providing some historical
and archaeological settings. In order of importance, these take the
form of a study of the chronology of the ossuaries and of a preface
to the whole book on the historical environment of the Judaeo-
Christians. There are pages of dense material, for the most part
completely new. Thence it transpires that Jewish Christian thought
continued from the beginning of the Church down till the end of the
fourth century... always associated with certain particular
practices." [31]

On the same subject, Daniélou had stated: "In a long introduction, Fr. Bagatti writes the history of this Jewish Christianity of
Palestine for the first time." [32] In this lengthy prologue, Bagatti's
aim was to fit the material gathered by Testa into its historical and
geographical framework. In a word, *Il simbolismo* was a study of
the Judaeo-Christians' teachings, usages and ways of expressing
their belief, together with other elements proper to their culture
and mentality. It was necessary to show that, contrary to common
belief, the Judaeo-Christians did not live on merely to 70 or 135
A. D. but to a much later time still.

---

30   G. Cardinal Pizzardo. Letter published in *LTS* 39 (1963), 15.
31   L. Moraldi, in *Rivista Biblica* 11 (1963), 201-202.
32   J. Daniélou, in *Recherches de Science Religieuse* 51 (1963), 117-121.

What was said in the introduction to Testa's book was well received and there were requests for a more detailed study of the Jewish Christian Church. Bagatti had already assembled much historical material on this subject. He decided to have it printed, enriching it with the description of archaeological remains brought to light by Testa.

There were also many requests that the author would make this volume available to people interested in Jewish Christianity but who were not necessarily specialists. Such requests came from friends and admirers who had previously been given hints about this new study. Thus there appeared L'Eglise de la Circoncision,[33] written in a simple style and easily obtainable. It represents a documented synthesis of the history and the archaeological monuments of the Jewish Christian Church.

Contents of the book.

The book was published in French for a variety of reasons, amongst others the fact that, being printed in the Near East, it would circulate more freely in cultural circles. Besides, there was already to hand a work in Italian, Il simbolismo by Testa. In his book, Bagatti first sets out the historical facts which prove that a Christian community of Jewish origin was in existence, and that it stood aloof from that of Gentile background for many centuries. He goes on to study the proselytizing practices of the Judaeo-Christians amongst the "lost sheep of Israel" (Matthew 10 :6).

Bagatti assembled information from the Talmud dealing with the Minim, heretics for Jews but believers for Christians. He weighed the various arguments and then concluded that, whatever some scholars had said hitherto, the theology of the Minim was, in general,

---

33   B. Bagatti, L'Eglise de la Circoncision. Translated by A. Storme according to the Italian manuscript. Jerusalem, 1965. Pp. 286, with illustrations.

the teaching of the Judaeo-Christians.

Light had been thrown on the Talmud controversies between the *Minim* and the rabbis from various angles by modern scholars. In his book on the Church of the Circumcision, Bagatti lists all the references chronologically.This is done in accord with the times when the rabbis, mentioned in the Talmud, had lived. All was set out geographically, too, according to the localities where the rabbis had dwelt.

Bagatti is aware that when the documents mention *Minim* these latter are not be identified always with Judaeo-Christians. Therefore, he discards certain references which are not clear and takes as his basis observations and facts which clearly evidence a body of Christian teaching. Nevertheless, he has been able to give us an idea of the way of life, the thought and the ideals aimed at by the Judaeo-Christians.

Since he is an archaeologist, Bagatti had to dedicate one part of his study to the buildings used by the Judaeo-Christians. The church-synagogue of Nazareth and that of Zion had their own interest. The signs and symbols used by Judaeo-Christians to express their religious beliefs were presented by the author in panoramic fashion and from the archaeological viewpoint. Similarly, he dealt with the Jewish Christian practices regarding initiation into their religion and those relative to the dead.

In a word, the book is a basic text, enriched with a generous bibliography on Jewish Christian studies. Closely reading this work, archaeologists will realize that we have to hand a body of material belonging to another culture, that it is different from that already known as deriving from the Gentile-Christian stream of Christianity and that the Church of the Circumcision was not as insignificant as was commonly believed.

Rightly can we conclude that the Church was formerly an entity to be reckoned with both from the numerical and moral viewpoints. Proofs of this are to be found in the evidence of *Acts* (4:4

and 21:20), the debates between the *Minim* and the rabbis, the growth of a school with its own special theological currents (later to conflict with that of the "Great Church"), the abundance of literature produced (enduring down to our own times), and the ossuaries found in various areas.

In this work, too, Bagatti has followed his own method. This consists in taking into account not only the stylistic characteristics of the monument under consideration, to the neglect of literary data, as sometimes can be seen in current archaeological publications, but first in setting the monument in its own literary context. This is the method he followed when dealing with the mosaics of Palestine. He is convinced that this is the only way to explain the respective archaeological finds. On the other hand, to judge a work of ancient art by modern standards is to commit an anachronism. Perhaps, this is why many students of Christian archaeology find it difficult to follow Bagatti's scholarship. They are loathe to abandon that critical method which would judge all Christian archaeological discoveries according to the ideology of that Church which sprang solely from Gentile sources.

Liturgists, too, may run into difficulties with Bagatti's methods. It is usual to date prayers, if not by means of their composition at least according to their official entry into the ancient liturgy as evidenced by the antiquity of the codices. On the other hand, they find in Bagatti's work that the prayers are studied and judged solely with respect to the ideas they contain. Thus, for example, the Offertory of the Requiem Mass, "Domine Jesu Christe," about which so much ink has flowed, is studied without reference to the codices but in the light of the ideas it expresses relative to the "cosmic ladder." It is thus correlated with other texts which speak of this "cosmic ladder" and with the monuments which depict it. Seen in this light and within this current of ideas, the text of the Offertory prayer in question is fully understood. Without further ado, we can conclude that it is very ancient, even though the codices do not make clear just how old it is. In fact, we cannot explain how it came into the liturgy unless its concepts had been understood by at least a considerable number of the faithful.[34]

The same can be said of the prayers which the liturgy prescribes for the "Commendation of Souls." In deciding whether this last document really originates with St. Peter Damian, one would have to investigate its ideas relative to the life to come.

Another idea commonly held by scholars was that all the Judaeo-Christians were Ebionites and that only with the Council of Nicea (325) did they come to believe explicitly in the divinity of Christ. In Bagatti's book, there is definite proof to the contrary. Symbols referring to Christ are described and it is seen that many signs express the idea that Christ was held to be God. Following in Testa's footsteps, Bagatti shows the evolution of such symbols as, for example, the "Constantine Monogram" and the "monogram cross." Their meaning was originally based on numbers, but their later development, on letters. The reference to Christ, however, remained constant.

The novelty of the book does not therefore lie in the presentation of hitherto unedited material. This the author has avoided with a view to making the work of examining such material easier for the specialists. Rather, the book is new because it interprets material largely known and edited already, fitting it into a stream of ideas acknowledged to be doctrinal.

Criticisms and opinions of the experts.

The novelty of the work was noted and appreciated almost immediately. The Dominican, Léon Ramlot, in an article on St. Justin described the book as "one of this year's most significant." [35] In

---

34 B. Bagatti, *LEC*, 160. "Le idee dei sette cieli," in *LTS* 39 (1963), 8-10.
35 L. Ramlot, "Un saint laïc: Justin Martyr," in *Bible et vie chrétienne* no 67 (1966), 78.

Germany, Philip Seidensticker gave it prominent notice.[36] Amongst other things, he says that the book "opens a new road in the almost unknown world of Jewish Christianity in Palestine." Rinaldi[37] examined the work within the author's own special field and wrote: "The new book is the work of a scholar who, in his own science (the archaeology of the Holy Land) is conscious of the help that the other well-known sciences can give. He is concerned to offer as instruments in their progress his own findings, together with the discoveries of objects already known, even outside Palestine, but now re-examined and brought together in the new collection of documents. The most remarkable advantages accrue to history and Christian art, in which the author is especially interested. But, through these two sciences, a contribution is also made to the exegesis of the New Testament, the history of ancient Christian literature, and to the symbolic expression of currents of thought, the fruits of which reach down to our own times. Not the least advantage of the book is that, side by side with a perfect control of the subject-matter, it offers an orderly portrayal thereof. If cannot be charged that this is a haphazard combination of different and unrelated elements. The data are distinct from the applications and, in the applications, the statements are separate from the theories."[38] Rinaldi concludes by saying that "the French translation, done with great devotion by A. Storme in Jerusalem, has bestowed on the text the freshness of something original."

Sofia Cavalletti[39] stresses "the abundance of material" relative to the symbols. She states that the work of Bagatti and Testa has, for years, gone on together, one mutually influencing the other. "The

36 Ph. Seidensticker, in *Franziskanische Studien* 48 (1966), 180-181.
37 G. Rinaldi, in *Bibbia e Oriente* 7 (1965), 263-264.
38 *Idem, art. cit.*, 264.
39 S. Cavalletti, in *Studi e materiali di Storia delle Religioni* 37 (1966), 125-128.

system they follow is that of researching the most ancient literary sources indubitably Jewish Christian in origin for episodes which illustrate and explain the symbols which archaeology is, little by little, bringing out of the ground. In this way, Bagatti and Testa have succeeded in reconstituting the soul which lies behind the symbols graven on rock or clay. At the same time, light is thrown on many texts, often quite obscure, through the symbols which were, so to say, the illustrations thereof. Bagatti devotes many pages of his book to the interpretation of graffiti and designs, citing the texts which form the basis of his exposition. They can be considered an illustrated anthology of Jewish Christian passages."

The authoress goes on to make a comparison with the discoveries at present attracting attention. "At a time which is so fruitful in archaeological discoveries, one automatically seeks to establish some order of priority and importance amongst them. The task is plainly difficult and problematical. Yet, we do not think we are far from the truth when we assign the return to life of the Jewish Christian world a major place in the whole picture of such rediscovery. Perhaps, a kind of standard was set with the discoveries at Qumran. They made known to us the way of life of a particular Jewish sect. Yet, it was still a small sector of life in Palestine at the time of Christ. The resurrection of the Jewish Christian world means that the germinal life of the Church itself has been made known to us." [40]

The Israeli writer, M. Tagliacozzo, [41] notes the author's objectivity. "Of the many studies which have appeared during the past decade and which are in some way of interest to the history of the Palestinian *yishuv* in the Mishnah-Talmudic period, this work by Fr. Bagatti has the rare value of not being restricted to partisan sources. Instead, the author, with scholarly intent, has been able

---

40   *Idem, art. cit.,* 127.
41   M. Tagliacozzo, in *La Rassegna mensile di Israel* XXXV (1969), 49.

to avail himself of all extra-Christian sources (*Mishnah*, the twofold *Talmud* and *Midrashim*) even when they might represent points of difference with the apologetic of the Fathers. Only rarely can it be said that historical endeavour of such complexity fills a gap in the field both of Jewish historiography and of primitive Christianity."

Daniélou's interest in the book was mainly from the angle of Patrology and he wrote a careful review. [42] He states that, in his own works he had established the fact that the Jewish Christian Church was in existence through the first centuries. Fr. Bagatti, on the other hand, presents data which prove that this community lived on to the fifth century, since the monuments he studied belong to this period. The Jesuit scholar stresses the fact that the archaeological documentation, now first assembled, shows the continuity of Jewish Christianity from the third to the fifth century. Precisely for this reason, Fr. Bagatti's work "endows Church history with a new dimension." Daniélou attaches importance to the book for the additional reason that it throws light on the history of relationships between Judaism and Christianity and on the story of Islamic origins.

A. Hamman, O. F. M. [43] reviewed the work from the same angle of Patrology. He stated that, for several years, studies on Jewish Christianity have been increasing and that books on the subject had been written by Schoeps and Goppelt in Germany and by Culmann and Daniélou in France. However, Bagatti's contribution has no relationship with anything previous for it deals with Jewish Christianity in the light of epigraphical and archaeological documents. The reviewer ends by saying that we owe a debt of gratitude to the two Franciscan scholars for their having given us "not more or less brilliant theories but the witness of stone which, in many cases, throws light on centuries of Christian history."

42   J. Daniélou, in *Recherches de Science Religieuse* 55 (1967), 92-96.
43   A. Hamman, in *Mélanges de Science Religieuse* 23 (1966), 241-242.

Bagatti's work was reviewed by experts in the biblical field
also. Thus, R. Le Déaut [44] writes that, all things considered, Fr.
Bagatti's book will be well received "for the new elements it contributes towards a rediscovery of a world that was lost, as also
for the wise interpretations it proposes. This is but a first summary
glance at the whole but the general lines laid down seem quite solid
in that they agree with the literary data. To edit this story there is
need of 'reintegrations,' exactly as has to be done with a mutilated
text. In any case, the specialists (palaeographers, archaeologists,
exegetes, historiographers, patrologists and liturgists) each attracted
by the respective subjects treated must acknowledge what has been
solidly established — free from partisanship. The task is too important and complex. Summary judgments on the part of specialists
will not do." [45]

This last phrase of Déaut's seems to be aimed at those who
had delivered summary assessments of Bagatti's studies on Jewish
Christian finds. We have already quoted de Vaux. Here we recall
another criticism which Audet [46] had written in connection with

---

44 R. Le Déaut, "La symbolique judéo-chrétienne," in *Biblica* 47 (1966),
283-289.

45 *Idem, art. cit.* It seems to me that E. Cothenet expresses the same idea
in his review of *Les premiers chrétiens* by A. Jaubert published in *L'Ami
du Clergé* 78 (1968), 264. He writes: "It is disappointing that the strict
limits of the collection did not allow Miss Jaubert to show us those Jewish
Christian communities of the first centuries to whom the works of Frs.
Daniélou and Bagatti have rightly drawn attention."

46 J. P. Audet, in *Revue Biblique* 69 (1962), 619-626. M.B. writes, in *Proche-
Orient Chrétien* 10 (1960), 373, relative to *Gli scavi del "Dominus Flevit"*:
"Of all these numerous tombs, is there not one or other which may be
Christian? The author points out one of them, no. 79, which contained
a certain number of ossuaries. By reason either of the names or of certain signs they would appear to be Christian. We must acknowledge that
we do not feel ourselves competent to assess the worth of these arguments."

Daniélou's *Les symboles chrétiens primitifs* in which the author took the finds by the Franciscans as his basis relative to the dating and origin of the documents. Audet stated: "So far as the date and provenance of the Palestinian archaeological documents are concerned, and there is question of these in several places in the discussion (pp. 44, 73, 103-115), it is only prudent to wait for new data before changing what is simply possible into the probable and the certain."

The reviews by Hamman, Daniélou and Déaut stated that the material published by Bagatti and Testa could already be used in the study of the Bible and Church History. Lino Randellini follows this out in a long article which was later expanded into a small book. He maps out a historical synthesis of the Church of the Circumcision. [47] Without feeling fully tied down, he presents the appropriate material, recalls the attitude of this Church when it came into contact with Jews as well as Gentile Christians, and gives the reasons why it died out. The rich information provided by Randellini presents a new and more developed view of what Bagatti and Testa had merely hinted at. He acknowledges his use of the material gathered in Jerusalem, for he considers it important. He writes: "... it is beyond doubt that they have opened up new paths to science. Palaeographers, archaeologists, exegetes, historians, patrologists and liturgists will be able to polish the conclusions of Bagatti and Testa but they cannot do less than record their gratitude for the task accomplished by them. Some slight adornments on what they have built may fall away but it is my impression that the mass of the structure shows itself more and more solid as time passes." [48]

47   L. Randellini, "La Chiesa della Circoncisione e la sua storia," in *Studi Francescani* 64 (1967), 13. Published as a separate booklet: *La Chiesa dei Giudeo-cristiani*. Brescia, 1968, 72.

48   *Idem, art. cit.*, 13.

Randellini states expressly that he does not wish to do a review nor to make a summary of Bagatti's work. However, since the main lines of his article are chiefly biblical, he selects such material as will serve his purpose: that of editing a short history of the Jewish Christian Church and mapping out its main stages from the beginning until its disappearance.

Francisco Uricchio,[49] Conventual Franciscan, examined the book from the biblical viewpoint also. He concluded: "We are persuaded that he has put into scholars' hands something for which we should be deeply grateful, a work which is quite solid and quite indispensable for those who work on the symbolic language transmitted on the monuments and in the epigraphy illustrated." He adds that the Judaeo-Christians are usually referred to in connection with the exegesis of passages of the New Testament, that there is talk of "the Judaizers," and that all is done in polemic fashion and in a cramped way. Uricchio holds that Bagatti's work "is important because it makes clear the reactions of the Jewish society to the Christian revelation. First in the order of time, these reactions are naturally and necessarily different from those of the Graeco-Roman culture. They therefore represent the first assimilation of the Christian message according to the lines of thought and the figurative language which was inherited from the Judaism of the time." [50]

Giovanni Garbini [51] reviewed the book from the archaeological viewpoint. He states that the finds of material belonging to the first Christian communities in Palestine are becoming ever more frequent. They make known the particular features of these communities which differ notably from other Christian communities of

---

49 F. Uricchio, in *Miscellanea Francescana* 67 (1967), 213-215.
50 *Idem, art. cit.*, 214.
51 G. Garbini, in *Oriens Antiquus* 5 (1966), 300-302.

Gentile origin. The writer styles as masterly the way Bagatti deals with such a difficult subject and reaches such satisfactory conclusions.

He analyses the first part of the book and then goes on to speak of the reasons behind the symbolism. He states that the religious symbolism in question is rich and complex and that is largely attested by texts mainly of a funerary nature attributed to the Judaeo-Christians. The writer admits that the great development of symbolism constitutes a singular phenomenon, having its roots deep in the culture of Jewish society which was generally opposed to the use of graven images.

Garbini then states that the phenomenon was not limited to Palestine only, but that there is question of an "enormous influence of un-rational, mystical thought which developed in the East through many centuries and then returned to the West in the first centuries of the Christian era either with the Gospel message or, still more so, with the Eastern religions like Mithraism." He stresses the particular feature (though perhaps it is not exclusively Jewish) which consists in attributing special meanings and powers to letters of the alphabet and to numbers. For the reviewer, Bagatti's work leaves people convinced "and perhaps a little disconcerted by the extent of Jewish Christian symbolism."

He underlines the fact that some symbols (as Bagatti had himself noted) have their origin in Mesopotamia and are sometimes definitely Sumerian. He finds interesting what the author has to say about the seven-branched candlestick which, though a purely Jewish symbol, is also found on Jewish Christian monuments. Finally, Garbini notes that the literary texts reproduced give a sure basis for the interpretation of the symbols.

Michelini Tocci's most recent book [52] deals with the Ebionites.

---

52   F. Michelini Tocci, *I manoscritti del Mar Morto*. Bari, 1967, 35.

In it the reader is referred to *L'Eglise de la Circoncision*. Paul Sacchi[53] in a review of Brandon's "Jesus and the Zealots" in *Revue de Qumran* also makes mention of Bagatti's work as the writer attempts to assess the legal problem which separated the first Christians. I. H. Dalmais, O. P.,[54] reviewing Bagatti's book, states that for years the problem of the Judaeo-Christians has been the subject of much research and that the studies and archaeological finds have not yet dissipated all uncertainty. Still they have made available so much new material that at least a provisional synthesis is possible. Credit is due Bagatti for having placed so many documents at the disposal of scholars and for having stimulated them to undertake that research which is so important for an exact knowledge of primitive Christianity and for an accurate assessment of the traditions which came in later.

4. *New studies on Dura - Europos.*

Dr. J. L. Teicher, the noted Jewish scholar, has an interesting article in *The Jewish Quarterly Review*.[55] The essay takes up only ten pages, including the fairly numerous footnotes. The very title, "Ancient Prayers in Hebrew" leads us to expect something new.[56] There is question of three fragments in Hebrew, found during the excavations at Dura-Europos, an ancient Mesopotamian city on the left bank of the Euphrates, midway between Aleppo and Bagdad. It was a Greek-Macedonian colony from 280 B.C. onwards until it

---

53 P. Sacchi, in his review of Brandon's *Jesus and the Zealots* in *Revue de Qumran* no. 23, February, 1968, 450.

54 I. H. Dalmais, in *Bible et Terre Sainte*, no. 92 (1967), 23.

55 J. L. Teicher, "Ancient Eucharistic Prayers in Hebrew," in *The Jewish Quarterly Review* 54 (1963-1964), 99-109.

56 I. Mancini, "Preghiere eucaristiche dei giudeo-cristiani," in *LTS* 40 (1964), 355-358.

passed to the Parthians in the following century. In 116 A.D. it was conquered by the Romans who stayed on until 256. In that year the Persians took it and destroyed it. The sands of the desert did the rest, gradually invading and covering everything. The ruins of Dura-Europos remained thus buried until 1920. From then until 1937 many archaeological excavations were carried out on the site.

Fig. 31. Dura Europos; a liturgical fragment of Eucharistic Character (from *JQR* 1963-64, p. 109).

Of the three Hebrew fragments found in the ruins of the synagogue there, one, in its present condition, is not of importance. It is very small and shows only a few letters. The other two have longer texts though they are mutilated at the beginning and the end of lines.

The two fragments had already been interpreted by C. C. Torrey [57] who took them to be parts of the one original text. According to Torrey's preliminary version, there is question of a Hebrew

57 C. C. Torrey, in *The Excavations at Dura-Europos, Preliminary Report*, VI. New Haven, 1936, 417-419.

140

liturgical text, a kind of thanksgiving after meals. Later, following remarks by Teicher, Torrey sought another and more satisfactory interpretation. Taking as his basis the last lines of the first fragment (where, in his translation, there is mention of eating animal meats), he thought of a formal text composed especially for the Jews who lived in Dura-Europos. In the third century, they were forbidden to kill animals and lived amongst their Gentile neighbours as vegetarians. In other words, according to Torrey, the text of the two fragments seems to be connected with the custom of eating animal foods. In concise terms, the documents stress the fact and provide authorization for the Jewish practice, this being contrary to what the rest of the Dura-Europos population followed.

Torrey's first interpretation, that of prayers after meals, was adopted unhestitatingly by Du Mesnil du Buisson [58] who also published an article interpreting the two fragments and adding pictures of the Dura-Europos synagogue.[59] Du Mesnil, while following Torrey, published additional details which do not seem quite worthy of credence. In fact, he supposed that there was a kind of restaurant close by the synagogue where Jews could find food allowed them by their law and where they could recite ritual prayers after eating. He wrote "It seems to us that Jews who were travelling and lodged in the synagogue could find suitable meals together with the ritual formulae to be read after dining. Such is the meaning of the liturgical document discovered there."[60]

Teicher has observed that the interpretation by Torrey and Du Mesnil, and the meaningless nature of their translation, make it

---

58 R. Du Mesnil Du Buisson, "Un parchemin liturgique juif et la gargote de la synagogue à Doura-Europos," in *Syria* (1939), 23-34.

59 R. Du Mesnil Du Buisson, *Les peintures de la synagogue de Doura-Europos*. Rome, 1939.

60 *Idem*, "Un parchemin liturgique juif et la gargote de la synagogue à Doura-Europos," in *Syria* 20 (1939), 28.

clear that they did not really succeed in identifying the nature of the fragments found in the synagogue. Teicher adds that this misunderstanding is due, not so much to the intrinsic difficulty of the Hebrew text, as to the preconceived ideas of the two scholars convinced as they were that they were dealing with two Jewish texts simply because they were written in Hebrew.

Prayers of Christian origin.

On the other hand, Teicher categorically claims that the two fragments found at Dura-Europos are Christian in origin because they are intimately related to the Eucharistic prayers of *Didache* 10, 3-4. *Didache* or *The Teaching of the Apostles* was very well known to Christians of the first centuries and was held in high regard by Church writers. In his *Ecclesiastical History* Eusebius mentions it after the Sacred Scriptures.[61] St. Athanasius,[62] having listed the canonical books, adds that there are other works which, though not included in the Canon itself, should be read by anyone who wished to be spiritually informed in accordance with the thought of the Fathers. Amongst such writings he names *Didache*.

For Christians of Jewish background, *Didache* must have been more precious still for its author was certainly a Judaeo-Christian and its country of origin was Syria or, more probably, Palestine itself. Teicher ends his article by pointing out some important conclusions which it delivers. "In the first place, the existence of a Christian eucharistic prayer in Hebrew, which cannot be later than the second half of the third century, indicates that Hebrew was used as a liturgical and ecclesiastical language in the Church during the first centuries. This finding is corroborated first, by the fact that the Hebrew of *Exodus* was read in the Church at Sardis, as

---

61 *Historia Ecclesiastica* III, xxv, 4 (*PG* 20, 269).
62 *Epist.* xxxix (*PG* 26, 1437).

mentioned in the Paschal Homily of Bishop Melito of Sardis; second, by the fact, on which I still insist, that the Dead Sea Scrolls, which are written in Hebrew, are of Christian origin; and finally, by the fact that Hebrew was used in early Christian tomb inscriptions, as I will show on another occasion."[63]

Whatever the worth of the second statement on the origin of the Qumran scrolls, it is certain that Teicher's conclusions are not so disconcerting since we know that a Jewish Christian community did exist even in Dura-Europos. In this connection, Bagatti had already stressed the identity of two symbols found at Dura-Europos and those discovered at "Dominus Flevit." He had insisted that a Jewish community must have been found there in Mesopotamia right from the beginning of Christian times, set up by the first Jewish disciples. [64] Testa[65] also underlined the Christian character of some signs found at Dura-Europos and compared them with identical symbols discovered elsewhere and which are certainly of Jewish Christian origin.

The finding of these Eucharistic prayers at Dura-Europos is of special worth since it helps us to understand another feature of Jewish Christian religious life, that of their faith and practice relative to the Eucharist. Besides Teicher's conclusions confirm the fact that Jewish Christianity had spread to cities far from Jerusalem.

63 J. L. Teicher, "Ancient Eucharistic Prayers in Hebrew," in *The Jewish Quarterly Review* 54 (1963-1964), 108.

64 B. Bagatti, *Gli scavi del "Dominus Flevit,"* 170.

65 E. Testa, *ISGC*, 379, no. 2, and p. 403, no. 1; see also pp. xxvii-xxviii.

Christian artists

The review *Syria* [66] had another surprise for us. There was a well-documented article by Count Du Mesnil du Buisson, already mentioned. Previously, he had studied and described various Christian symbols found at Dura-Europos.[67] Thanks to his precision in reproducing well-studied material, he has provided a valuable repertory for Christian archaeologists. Many of the symbols in question must be related to Jewish Christian teaching. This is now familiar to scholars, thanks to the writings of Daniélou and the Franciscans of "The Flagellation."

The new work by Du Mesnil is of special interest since, in a way, it brings to light the culture and social standing of the Judaeo-Christians of Dura-Europos. We know that the city was destroyed in 256. For this reason, the documents are important for a well-dated period. Another reason is that they reveal another Christian element in the synagogue of Dura-Europos.

The subject dealt with by the author is summed up in the title of his article, "L'inscription de la niche centrale de la synagogue de Doura-Europos." It is well known that the central niche where was exhibited the cupboard or the ark containing the Torah scrolls was considered the most sacred part of the synagogue. Visitors to the Damascus museum can still see the synagogue of Dura-Europos for it was removed and reconstructed there. They can admire the niche in the middle front wall. It is covered with pictures representing (centre) the facade of the Jerusalem Temple, (right) the

---

66 R. Du Mesnil Du Buisson, "L'inscription de la niche centrale de la synagogue de Doura-Europos," in *Syria* 40 (1963), 303-314. I. Mancini, "Un artista cristiano nella sinagoga di Dura-Europos," in *LTS* 41 (1965), 171-174.
67 R. Du Mesnil Du Buisson, "Sur quelques signes chrétiens," in *Rivista di Archaeologia cristiana* 23-24 (1947-1948), 313-325; also in *Mélanges de l'Université de Saint-Joseph* 36 (1959), 1-49.

144

Fig. 32. Dura Europos:
Niche in the Synagogue
where is found the
graffito of Sisa, a
Christian Artisan (from
LTS 1965, p. 173).

sacrifice of Abraham and (left) the seven-branched candlestick.
The inscription-graffito studied in the article in question is found
exactly in the apparently empty space under the candlestick. This
graffito had been studied by the author in 1939, but he was not
successful in reading and translating it completely. Another interpretation by Kraeling in 1965, though faulty, is much nearer the

truth.[68]

Du Mesnil made a fresh study of the inscription and, after considering all the possibilities, offered this translation of the graffito: "Martin who executed the work (the picture) in the cupboard niche (*beit 'arōn*) and Sīsā (who fashioned) the form of the holy cupboard (,arōn haqōdeš)." [69]

The writer states that the two names, Martin and Sīsā, represent the two artists, the first being the painter who adorned the niche with figures and decorations, the second being responsible for the ark to contain the Torah scrolls.

Du Mesnil's further remarks may be noted. He says that the painter who worked on the central niche at Dura-Europos may have been the first to decorate a synagogue with figures. He did it with a certain hesitation and discretion. Since there was question of a first attempt, he did not wish to offend the sensibilities of Jews brought up on the rabbinic tradition. Hence, he avoided depicting Abraham and Isaac from the front. Besides, the differences between these pictures and those which adorn the rest of the synagogue give reason to think that this Martin confined himself to decorating the central niche while other artists did the remaining paintings.

Regarding the person responsible for the cupboard, Sīsā by name, Du Mesnil says that he was a Christian and identifies him with the artist who worked in the Dura-Europos baptistery. In support of this, the author brings forward these points: (a) the same name. One of the artists who had left his signature in the baptistery was called precisely "Siseos" (a Hellenized transcription of *Sys*). He adds the qualification, "the humble" to his name, and asks

68   C. H. Kraeling, *The Synagogue*. New Haven, 1956, p. 269. B. 2, Plate 78.
69   R. Du Mesnil Du Buisson, "L'inscription de la niche centrale de la synagogue de Doura-Europos," in *Syria* 40 (1963), 310.

to be remembered before Christ; [70] (b) the same period. Both the baptistery and the synagogue at Dura-Europos go back to the first half of the third century; (c) the rarity of the name. Siseos was an uncommon name at Dura-Europos. This reason, taken with the preceding, carries weight. Actually, we cannot easily conceive a coincidence between two distinct persons with the same rare name, following the same profession and living at the same time in the one city.

At the end of his article, Du Mesnil asks why the signature of the two artists in the central niche, so accurately set in the space below the candlestick, was not more firmly done, and why it did not remain visible. The reason given by the writer confirms his interpretation of the graffito. He maintains that the rabbis of the synagogue must have remained very susceptible and must have been opposed to the fact that when their faithful prayed in this place they would have had continually before their eyes the names of two individuals who were not Jews and one of them almost certainly a Christian. The names were inscribed in the most holy spot of all, side by side with symbols of the pure Jewish faith. [71]

Before ending these notes on the recent finds of material of Christian origin in Dura-Europos, we wish to draw attention once more to the importance of these discoveries. They show the relationships which existed in the city between the Judaeo-Christians and the Jews. Besides, they help us understand, to some extent, the Jewish mentality itself and they help solve the problem of the synagogue.

---

70   C. E. Hopkins, *The Excavations at Dura-Europos. Preliminary Report V*, pp. 241-242.

71   R. Du Mesnil Du Buisson, "L'inscription de la niche centrale de la synagogue de Doura-Europos," in *Syria* 40 (1963), 314.
      11 (1960-1961), 288-314.

The other matter, namely, the fact that the artist responsible for the holy cupboard was a Christian allows us to see in a new light the conclusions already reached by Teicher, a Jewish scholar, regarding the Christian nature of the synagogue. If a non-Jewish artist like Martin and a Judaeo-Christian like Sīsā worked there together, certain anomalies can be explained. Whether the synagogue itself was a place of worship for the Jewish Christian community of Dura-Europos is another question. To be sure, the problem is already stated and other finds like those of Teicher and Du Mesnil will open the way towards a definite solution.

5. *Studies of other places.*

To broaden their knowledge of the Church of the Circumcision, Bagatti and Testa undertook journeys to different places where it might be expected that Judaeo-Christians had lived. First, they visited areas closer to Jerusalem and some villages of Galilee. Later, they studied districts in Syria and Asia Minor, paying special attention to the lands of the Seven Churches of the Apocalypse. Rome itself was not forgotten, seeing that it would surely have played host to a community of Judaeo-Christians. This research has allowed the scholars to form a more or less approximate idea of the development and influence of the Jewish Christian Church during the first years of Christianity.

Towns divided in two.

Bagatti [72] throws light on some places in Palestine, taking as his basis the information provided by ancient writers, especially St. Epiphanius. The Jewish sources call such villages "those swallowed up," that is, lost to the Land of Israel. Some of them were

---

72 B. Bagatti, "Ricerche su alcuni antichi siti giudeo-cristiani," in *LA* 11 (1960-1961), 288-314.

occupied by Judaeo-Christians. Taking account of such titles, and following the lines traced by Epiphanius, Eusebius and the Talmud (on debates between *Minim* and the rabbis), Bagatti has been able to draw a kind of geographical map which allows one to see the centres where Judaeo-Christians lived.

It is known that these latter dwelt in the same places as Jews but, by reason of the *habdala* or "separation" in a quarter of the town apart from those faithful to the synagogue, as if in a kind of ghetto. When visiting Ba'ina in Galilee, [73] Bagatti was guided by such literary data and actually found that the village, one of those "swallowed up," was evenly divided into two parts, like two adjacent settlements, both bearing the same name. Elsewhere, on the other hand, he found the remains of two synagogues, for example, at el-Jish, ancient Jiscala, [74] and Kefr Kenna, [75] still held to be ancient Cana. The presence of two synagogues in the one town shows that it was inhabited by two separate communities. From our present point of view we can say that the two were comprised of Jews who remained faithful to the synagogue and those who had become Judaeo-Christians.

Bagatti states that the style of the synagogues of Galilee is well known. It reaches back to classical art but with the addition of decorative motifs which are plainly Jewish, for example, the palm and the bunch of grapes — both favored by Jews as symbols of fecundity. In some places, like Shefa 'Amr, [76] these symbols are found even on tombs which also bear invocations of Christ. In such cases, it is clear that there is a continuity of the basic Jewish

73   B. Bagatti, "Ba'ineh, Villaggio Inghiottito," in *LTS* 41 (1965), 78-82.
74   B. Bagatti, "Giscala Cristiana," in *LTS* 39 (1963), 293-299.
75   B. Bagatti, "Le antichità di Kh. Qana e di Kefr Kenna in Galilea," in *LA* 15 (1964-1965), 290.
76   B. Bagatti, "Tradizione e arte a Shefa 'Amr in Galilea," in *LTS* 41 (1965), 180-187.

Fig. 33. View of Baniah, a "engulfed" village, from the south
(from *LTS* 1956 p. 76)

Fig. 34. A Cristian tomb of Shefaram, decorated with grape-vines
(from *LTS* 1965, p. 184)

culture but with new Christian elements. Later, in some localities like Sepphoris, the same Jewish motifs are changed, being conceived under a new light by the Judaeo-Christians.

These investigations of villages involved much time and work but they provided the scholars with an opportunity to bring to light and make a study of many finds of this kind. Though apparently of minor importance, they actually witness the presence of

Fig. 35. Kankabe in the region of Damascus (from *LA* XI, p. 279.).

the ancient Christian communities. Naturally, Galilee has, up to the present, provided the most numerous examples of Jewish Christian settlements. However, other areas show traces of such centres. For example, there still exists in Syria a village called "Kaukabe" ("the star") which corresponds to the locality where, according to

Epiphanius,[77] Ebionites and Nazarenes dwelt. An analytic study by Diez Merino [78] of the signs appended to the Nabatean inscriptions in Sinai shows that the Nabateans, also, had a certain relationship with Jewish Christian ideas. There we can see the cross with three horns, the cosmic and monogram crosses as also those ending in three triangles. There is also the tree of life, the star, and so on. Some Nabatean symbols correspond to those found in Jewish and Arabic works, but others, to those used only by Judaeo-Christians.

In the region of the Seven Churches of the Apocalypse, Bagatti and Testa found inscriptions, signs and objects which throw light on Jewish Christian teaching.[79] It is surprising that some signs are still used by folk of Palestine and can be seen traced on the walls of their homes, especially at the entrance. Is it guesswork to suppose that they derive from of old, relics of the Jewish Christian mentality ? It is commonly known that, in such matters, there is a traditional tenacity to transmit and preserve which defies explanation. It can be said that the more mysterious the teachings, the more confirmed is the tendency to guard them jealously.

In this regard, we may quote, for example, the experience of Colombano Chelveder[80] in Betsahur, a shepherds' village near Bethlehem. In one house, he was able to observe a granary made of beaten earth mixed with straw which had designs on its walls. They recalled symbols found elsewhere and which were of a Jewish Christian character. For example, there was the wavy line (symbol of life-giving water) and the cross in various forms(in the tree

---

77 *Adv. Haereses* I, ii, 29 and 30 (*PG* 41, 401-402 and 407-408).
78 P. Diez Merino, "Origen de los signos que acompañan a las inscripciones nabateas del Sinai," in *LA* 19 (1969), 264-304.
79 B. Bagatti, "Tracce giudeo-cristiane nella regione delle Sette Chiese dell'Apocalisse," in *LA* 12 (1961-1962), 177-220.
80 C. Chelveder, "Symboles chrétiens au village des Pasteurs," in *La Terre Sainte* 1964, 224-226.

of life, surrounded by water, in the shape of the Greek *Phi*, intertwined with an anchor, inscribed in the cosmos).

Many of these symbols which are still in use are common to both Christians and Moslems.[81] This is a clear sign that, even after many centuries, mystic religious iconography has changed but little. It is not easy to determine what the people make of such symbols for they are of an intimate, religious nature. First enquiries meet with only very vague answers. Only if one presses the point, and shows some signs of already being aware, will they confirm the interpretation offered by the visitor.

The light of the Gospel reached Rome directly from Jerusalem, directly through Peter and Paul. As a cosmopolitan city, it played host to faithful coming from all parts of the world. It was therefore to be expected that it would provide archaeological material pertinent to Jewish Christianity. Bagatti has studied this in a special article. [82]

Here, the author takes account of the literature which was contemporaneous and indigenous with the discoveries he examines. He states that many symbols in the more ancient catacombs like those of Priscilla, St. Callistus and Domitilla resemble those found on the ossuaries and the walls of funerary buildings in Jerusalem. They must be attributed to Judaeo-Christians. For that reason, they are to be explained in the light of Jewish Christian teaching. If no reference is made to Christ, then we can no longer pretend to explain such symbols as the plow, the ladder, the candelabrum, the water spurting from the arms of the monogram cross such as we see on the epitaph preserved at San Lorenzo in Verano.

---

81 T. Canaan, "Tâsit er-Radjfeh (Fear Cup)," in *The Journal of the Palestine Oriental Society* 3 (1923), 122-131.
    By the same author, "Arabic Magic Bowls," *ibid.* 16 (1936, 79-127; "Mohammedan Saints and Sanctuaries in Palestine," *ibid.*, 4 (1924), 32-33.
82 B. Bagatti, "Ricerche su alcuni segni delle Catacombe romane," in *LA* 15 (1964-1965), 98-123.

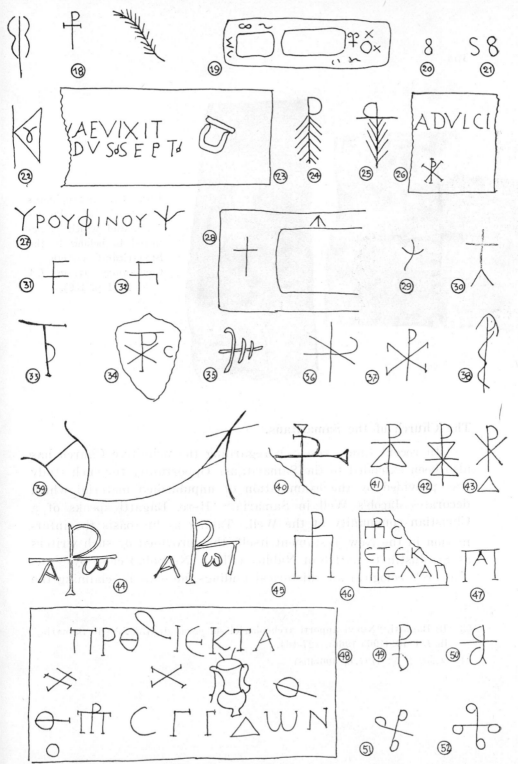

Fig. 36. Signs from Roman catacombs (from *LA* XV, p. 101).

Fig. 37. Sarcophagus preserved at Jacob's Well, and which is believed to belong to the Samaritan-Christian Community (from *LA* XVI p. 139).

The Church of the Samaritans.

In recent times, research regarding the primitive Church has also been extended to the Samaritans. Opportunity for such study was provided by the examination of unpublished material which decorates Jacob's Well in Samaria.[83] Here, Bagatti speaks of a Christian community at the Well. Taking as his basis the information in the New Testament itself, that provided by such writers as St. Justin (a native of Nablus (Flavia Neapolis) close by) [84] as also archaeological and historical findings, he ends by claiming the

---

83   B. Bagatti, "Nuovi apporti archeologici sul pozzo di Giacobbe in Samaria," in *LA* 16 (1965-1966), 127-164.

84   *Apol.* I, 53 (*PG* 6, 406-408).

existence of a Samaritan Christian Church with its own rites, including that of circumcision — exactly as in the case of the Judaeo-Christians who remained faithful to this practice.

Bagatti's statements in this regard are supported also by the witness of the Bordeaux Pilgrim. In 333, he found only a baptistery, without a church, at the Well. This is in accord with the rule followed by the Judaeo-Christians of not altering places by putting up buildings. Examples of this are to be found at the Holy Sepulchre, Bethany, the Tomb of the Virgin, and so on. In the pre-Constantine era, a baptistery without a church did not necessarily mean that the place was not regarded as a religious site. This has been proven by Bagatti in the case of Nazareth.

Further research will be rewarded with new finds and these will furnish more data for our knowledge of the Samaritan Christian Church — just as has already occurred in the case of the closely-affiliated Church of the Judaeo-Christians. In this regard, we may take account of the recent study by Stephen Yonick.[85] He came to the conclusion that the marble inscriptions found on Mount Nebo are the work of Samaritan Christians and that they date back to about the sixth century.

85 S. Yonick, "The Samaritan Inscription from Siyagha. A Reconstruction and Restudy," in *LA* 17 (1967), 162-221.

156

CHAPTER IV

THE MAIN RESULTS

It may seem that the discoveries relative to the Judaeo-Christians can interest the archaeologist only, that they can warm the heart only of some rare devotee of antiquities. Yet, they are meaningful on a much larger scale because of the results that have been achieved. These have reference to our knowledge of Church history, the study of the original shrines in Palestine, the new proofs provided in favour of their authenticity, and an appreciation of the mystic theological radiance which was thought to hover over them. They are meaningful, too, for modern ecumenism and for our endeavours to solve the problem of the primitive rite of the Jerusalem Church.

1. *Origin of the Christian shrines.*

First, there is the matter of proofs in favour of the genuineness of the shrines. Until about ten years ago, it was usual to begin looking for evidence in the Constantine and post-Constantine basilicas. In the majority of cases and with respect to the long period between Christ and Constantine, scarcely anything was alleged in the way of proof.[1]

---

1   This is borne out by a quick look at D. Baldi, *Enchiridion Locorum Sanctorum.* 1ed. Jerusalem, 1935; 2nd ed., Jerusalem, 1955. This book brings together all the then-known historical witnesses. Thus, it contains proofs emanating almost exclusively from Gentile-Christian authors. In view of this, the professors at the Franciscan House of Biblical Studies have in view the preparation of another volume which will bring together the Judaeo-Christian texts. These will describe the sanctuaries mainly according to the mystical "aura," against a theological background.

At present, in view of the new finds relative to the Jewish Christian Church, the problem is viewed differently. The Judaeo-Christians actually lived on in many of the localities sanctified by the presence of the Saviour. It is clear that they felt the urge to venerate these places out of devotion and to transmit the appropriate traditions down through the first three centuries. Thus, even from this viewpoint alone, the work of the scholars of the Franciscan House of Biblical Studies in Jerusalem, is in line with the activity of the Custody of the Holy Land which has gone on for hundreds of years in favour of the Holy Places. In other words, the specialists are providing a scientific basis for the genuineness of those many sites.

Double tradition on the shrines.

To understand adequately the traditions handed on by the Judaeo-Christians regarding local references to the life of Christ, it must be remembered that, in the majority of cases, the writings of Paul and Luke remained inaccessible. More than that, they were rejected out of hand because of their teaching on the negative value of the Mosaic Law and the practice of circumcision. This doctrine just did not fit in with the mentality of the Judaeo-Christians. With this in mind, we can readily understand why it is useless to look for Jewish Christian traditions on events reported solely by St. Luke. An example is the story of the raising of the widow's son in Naim. If these memories had not been transmitted by some other means, for example by local tradition, they would certainly have died out. On the other hand, episodes narrated by Matthew and John remained vividly alive because they were continually brought to mind by Gospel readings and the liturgy. It was only later that Gentile Christians retraced the topographical data left by Luke and were able to find other places made holy by the presence of the Redeemer. As is clear, the former memories have the advantage of being the more ancient and, consequently, the more certain.

158

To bring this home, we have but to think of the itinerary of the Bordeaux Pilgrim. He visited Palestine in 333, just as the Gentile-Christian movement was getting under way. Only three basilicas had as yet been erected on the sites of the sanctuaries. Without a local guide, well acquainted with all the Jewish Christian traditions (as the Pilgrim notes), it would have been impossible for him to have transmitted to us the detailed information we find in his itinerary. Thus, the guide on the spot could not have been anyone else but a Judaeo-Christian fully aware of the way things had evolved.

In other cases, the witnesses to tradition cited by Gentile-Christians are St. Cyril of Jerusalem and Eusebius, both contemporaries of the beginnings of the Gentile-Christian development in the Holy Land. Regarding Eusebius, we know that when he composed his *Onomasticon* or list of sacred places in Palestine, he sometimes based himself on the Bible, as a source, and at other times he refers to the practice of Christians of his time who continued to visit a spot and to pray there, thus preserving the memory of what had once occurred. This was the case, according to Eusebius, at Gethsemane, Bethany and Bethlehem.

A proof of this specification of localities on the part of the Judaeo-Christians relative to places sanctified by the Redeemer's life on earth (as also of their continued presence in some of them) is provided by Bagatti. [2] It involved a patient, accurate reconstruction, put together like a mosaic, based on many testimonies and resulting in the conclusions we have already mentioned.

This study of the origin of the shrine-traditions gave Bagatti an opportunity to observe how St. John associates Gospel episodes with the memory of water. The evangelist not only speaks of the Jordan, as the others had done, but also of Bethany in Trans-

2   B. Bagatti, "Le origini delle tradizioni dei Luoghi Santi in Palestina," in *LA* 14 (1963-1964), 32-64.

jordan (Jn 1:19-39), of Enon (where John was baptizing: Jn 3: 22-24), of the Probatic Pool (Jn 5:1-7), of Siloam in Jerusalem (Jn 9:1-7), of Jacob's Well (Jn 4:1-42), of the Lake (with the appearance to the apostles and the bestowal of the primacy on Peter: Jn 21:1-23) and of Cana (with the change of water into wine: Jn 2: 1-10). He mentions water even when there is no apparent need to do so as, for example, "the torrent" of Kidron, a valley where water is seen only in the rainy season (Jn 18: 1-12).

Let us hope that scholars will study the relationship which may exist between this tendency of St. John with his frequent allusions to water and certain Jewish Christian symbols of water found by the archaeologists.

The Jewish Christian apocrypha.

The contribution made by Jewish Christian studies to the genuineness of the shrine traditions is often based on the apocrypha, many of them written by Judaeo-Christians and reflecting their mentality. Actually, no one denies that these writings can be treated, at least sometimes, as historical or that they form theological documents of primary importance.

In this regard, Daniélou [3] observes that, amongst Jewish Christian works, Bagatti includes the *Story of Joseph the Carpenter* and the *Transitus Mariae*. "Relative to this last-mentioned work, Fr. Bagatti has elsewhere shown (*Rivista Biblica* 11 (1963), 38-52) that it must have had relationship with Jewish Christian worship at the tomb of the Virgin on Mount Olivet. There is no need to stress the importance of this for Jewish Christian origins of the dogma of the Assumption with regard both to its antiquity and its formulation."

3   J. Daniélou, in *Recherches de Science Religieuse* 55 (1967), 93.

The *Transitus Mariae* is already well-known, but it has been studied anew and it is found to show traces of Jewish Christian teaching. For instance, there is reference to the "cosmic ladder" when it speaks of the fear the Madonna felt when faced with the ascension, her prayer first to the archangel and then to Jesus for help. When this apocryphon fell into the hands of the Gentile-Christians, the passages which reflected Jewish Christian teaching were suppressed. Still, certain relics are found in some editions, showing the antiquity and true character of the latter. Examples of this are Pseudo-Melito (B1) and the Greek codex Vaticanus 1892 (R).

For us, study of this particular Jewish-Christian apocryphon is of great value because it provides data on the traditional Tomb of the Virgin in the Valley of Josaphat. There, some parts of the primitive tomb remain, dating back to the first centuries. When the fourth-fifth century monument was being built there was no question but that this tomb should be kept in its original shape. Thus, in Constantine's time, exactly the same thing occurred as in the case of the tomb of the Redeemer and the tombs of the martyrs in Rome.

The mystic character of three shrines.

Another result of studies of Jewish Christianity relative to the shrines is that these latter are now regarded in the light of the mystic halo or radiance which was thought to hover over them in the first centuries of Christianity. This idea is based on a type of devotion which was nourished by biblical texts drawn up under the title of *Testimonia*. To understand the mystic theological concept in question, a knowledge of the Testimonies taken from the Bible, and especially the apocalypses, is essential. The Testimonies drawn from the latter books were partially rejected by the Gentile-Christians, accustomed as they were to express their theological ideas according to the concepts and culture of the Graeco-Roman world.

Three places, especially, show clearly the above-mentioned mystical idea as developed by the Judaeo-Christians in their regard: Bethlehem, Mount Olivet and the Holy Sepulchre. They correspond to the three great aspects of Jesus' career: birth, teaching, death-resurrection.

This concept of mystic radiance in these three localities has been profoundly studied by Testa in a long article.[4] In it he describes the origin, development and evolution of the Mysteries which the Judaeo-Christians conceived as occurring there. Testa also deals with the pagan profanation of these places which was ordered by emperor Hadrian in 135. It was much more sacrilegious than we usually imagine for it meant the introduction of pagan worship, similar in expression but quite contrary theologically to what the first Christians had carried on there.

To understand the teaching which developed at these three shrines, it is essential to refer to the theories on "the mystery grottos." We already know that, for purposes of worship, the Judaeo-Christians of Palestine availed themselves not only of the synagogues but also developed their ritual in certain "sacred and mystic caves."[5] From a hint in one of Cyril of Jerusalem's sermons, we take it that this worship was still carried on by Judaeo-Christians in the fourth century.[6] Cyril actually recommends to foreign visitors visiting the Holy City that, when they want to find out where the "Lord's house" is, they should make their request explicit and enquire of "the Catholic Church," for the "sect of the impious" call their caves the Lord's house. Cyril's scarcely affectionate wording reflects the struggle which had been going on in the Holy Land

---

4   E. Testa, "Le 'Grotte dei Misteri' Giudeo-cristiane," in *LA* 14 (1963-1964), 65-144.
5   Eusebius of Caesarea, *De laudibus Constantini* IX (*PG* 20, 1369).
6   Cyril of Jerusalem, *Cat. XVIII*, 26 (*PG* 33, 1048).

162

between Gentile-Christians and the Church of the Circumcision for some ten years.

In the Church of Palestine, there was mention of "three holy and mystic caves," that is, the grotto of the Nativity, that under Golgotha and that of the Ascension — all three being conceived as "grottos of light" which had been reflected by the divinity entering there.

The mystic grotto of Bethlehem.

Regarding the grotto at Bethlehem, it had been venerated from the time of the apostles onwards. Therein, "in the silence of God" there were fulfilled two of the "three Mysteries" par excellence: that of Mary's virginity and her bringing forth. (The third of these mysteries is "the death of the Lord").[7] Because of its mysteries, the grotto of Bethlehem, though naturally dark, became one of the "most lightsome grottos."[8] In the minds of the Judaeo-Christians, the grotto of the Nativity was wholly bound up with the concept of light. At least three apocrypha, namely, *Pseudo Matthew, De Partu Virginis* and the *Protoevangelium of James* speak of the birth of Jesus in the cave of Bethlehem and describe the effulgence of light which filled the place. Thus, the birth of Christ from the Virgin Mary was always presented as a mystery of light.

The Judaeo-Christians had a deep devotion to the grotto of Bethlehem for another reason, that is, it represented the first "descent" of Christ. It is now certain that the teaching on the mystic grottos is bound up with the purely Jewish Christian doctrine of the "descent" and "ascent" of Christ and his initiated ones. Christ "descending" from heaven rested in Bethlehem "under the earth,"

---

7   Ignatius of Antioch, *Ad Eph*. XIX 2 (*PG* 5, 660).
8   For the terminology see *The Conflict of Adam and Eve* in Migne, *Dictionnaire des Apocryphes* I, 297 and 388.

as Eusebius says.[9] He remained "in an underground cave in which light had never been, but only darkness, for the light of day it had never known." [10]

Fig. 38. "very lucid" grotto of Bethlehem in a mosaic of the 12 century. (from *LA* XIV, p. 73).

Thus, Bethlehem was, for Judaeo-Christians, a "most light-some grotto." It is certain that Gregory of Nyssa was thinking of this when he told the faithful that the grotto in which the Lord was

9   Eusebius of Caesarea, *De vita Constantini* III, 43 (*PG* 20, 1001-1002).
10   Pseudo Matthew 13, 2. Cfr M.R. James, *The Apocryphal New Testament.* Oxford, 1953, 74.

born should make them ponder on the passage from the darksome, underground life of men to the illumination of the human race which came about through Christ.[11]

Testa, in the article we are speaking of, writes: "The Creed of Constantinople with the phrases 'Deum de Deo, *lumen de lumine, Deum verum de Deo vero*; natum, non factum.... Qui propter nos homines et propter nostram salutem *descendit* de coelis' re-echoes the Palestinian theology on the divine appearance at Bethlehem. Actually, it is thought to have been composed by St. Cyril, bishop of Jerusalem." [12]

For the Judaeo-Christians, the Bethlehem grotto became, as it were, a symbol of passage from darkness to light. Thus, for them, the town of Bethlehem came to stand for the Church of the Gentiles for, in the persons of the Magi to whom the star appeared, it understood the great mystery worked in God's silence when a star shone out in the heavens. On the other hand, Jerusalem was the symbol of the Church of the Circumcision.

For the mystery of Christ's birth, Hadrian substituted the mysteries of Tammuz, the Babylonian deity of vegetation, corresponding to Adonis in Greek mythology. The emperor had a wood planted exactly over the grotto where, in June-July, women in tears went down to bemoan the annual death of the god who was subsequently due to arise and ascend into heaven. Cyril of Jerusalem recalls this grove of Tammuz when he tells his catechumens: "Until these recent years, the place was covered with trees." [13]

St. Jerome who lived for thirty-three years in Bethlehem had certainly heard from the inhabitants that "from the time of Hadrian

---

11 *In diem Natalem Christi* (PG 46, 1141).
12 E. Testa, "Le 'Grotte dei Misteri' giudeo-cristiane," in *LA* 14 (1963-1964), 75.
13 *Cat. XII*, 20 (PG 33, 752).

until Constantine, our Bethlehem, the most revered place on earth, of which the psalmist sang, 'Truth has gone forth from the earth,' had been blotted out by Tammuz, that is, Adonis, and in the grotto where the Child Jesus had whimpered the lovers of Venus lamented." [14]

This profanation served to maintain the tradition of the place where Christ was born. About 248, Origen saw people still pointing out the Bethlehem grotto, so much so that the pagans were aware of the place where Jesus had been born.[15]

The mystic grotto of Calvary.

The other "mystic grotto" of the Judaeo-Christians was that which was situated under Calvary. Testa says that the Judaeo-Christians localized the "descent into hell" there. The crack in the rock (still visible today), the belief that Jerusalem was the hub of the world, the siting of Adam's grave there, the localizing there of the chief deeds of the Hebrew Patriarchs — all this contributed to the formation of a theology centering on the spot. It expressed truths of our faith in a much more concrete way than we are accustomed to now.

To bring out the idea of the redemptive work of Christ, the Judaeo-Christians felt it needful to create the legend around Calvary that Adam had been buried in the grotto below. The parallel, Adam-Christ, which is quite basic in St. Paul's theology of the redemption also, lies behind these narratives concerning Adam which evolved fully around Calvary. The second Adam was to make good all the damage brought about by the first, amongst which was death. Therefore, Christ's victory was to affect not only the devil and sin but also to bring about a triumph over death, snatching its prey away.

---

14   *Epist. LVIII* (PL 22, 581).
15   *Contra Celsum* I, 51 (PG 11, 756).

166

Fig. 39. Adam under
Calvary in a medie-
val minature of Va-
lenciennes, with de-
tail of Adam. (from
LTS 1965, p. 278)

The first to be rescued was, naturally, Adam. By his liberation, that of all humanity could well be expressed.

The tradition about Adam's burial under Calvary was gathered and transmitted by several Fathers of the Church. According to them, it derives from Jewish sources. These, in turn, must have been Christians also, for the synagogue held that Adam was buried at Hebron or on Mount Moriah.

The main source of this localization is the apocryphal work *The Book of the Conflict of Adam and Eve*, composed in the fifth or sixth century but containing much older elements. It tells us that Adam's first grave was in a grotto situated in the foothills of the earthly paradise. There he remained until after the Flood. At that time, Sem, Melchisedech and the angel Michael effected the transfer of his bones, carrying them by divine command to the place where the redemption would be wrought.

To stress the effects of the future redemption of the human race, the apocryphon asserts that the voice of the man who had first died guided the little funeral procession on its long journey. While they travelled, the voice kept repeating that, in the country to which they were being directed, the Word of God would come down. On the exact spot where the human remains were to be left, He would suffer and be crucified. Thus, the head of Adam would be bathed and purified in the blood of the Redeemer and, in this way, the salvation of Adam and all his posterity would be brought about.

Influenced by this idea, and in accord with St. Paul's text, "he descended into the lower regions of the earth" (Eph 4:9), the Judaeo-Christians spoke of the descent of Christ crucified into the grotto beneath Calvary (identified with Še'ol) to save Adam. It was through the great rent in Calvary's rock (caused by the earthquake mentioned in Matthew 27:51-52), Jesus would have made his "descent into hell."

In this connection, St. Irenaeus writes, "Three days he remained where the dead abode ... he went down to them to free and save them ...." [16] St. Cyril of Jerusalem [17] expresses the same idea, adding the detail that Christ went down to hell (*Še'ol*) under Calvary through the split in the rock that was still there. Through this opening the blood and water, flowing from the side of Christ crucified, would have reached the mortal remains of Adam and brought them back to life.

According to the author of *The Conflict of Adam and Eve*, this was the water sought by the first man. Driven from paradise, he had asked for *the water of life*. The reply was that this would not be given immediately, but on the day when the blood of God would be poured over his head.

The effects of the redemption brought about by Christ are described in concrete fashion as a return to the light, the setting free from prison, the liberation from darkness, the passions and from bonds of all kinds. Thanks to the coming (*descent*) of Christ, Adam could go out from 'the darksome grotto and climb the mountain illumined by rays of the true light."

Testa goes on to explain this mystic theological radiance created by the Judaeo-Christians around Calvary. According to their special ideas, the redemption by Christ was to have particular meaning for Adam: a kind of anticipated glorification of his body also. In this connection, we read in *The Conflict of Adam and Eve* that Melchisedech saw on the body of the first man a great light, while in the grotto under Calvary he could see angels going up and coming down to help the just souls scale the "cosmic ladder" between the grotto and paradise.

The angels in question are the "psychopompoi" ("soul-escorts") who, according to Jewish Christian teaching had the task of accompanying the souls of the just in their ascent of the "cosmic ladder," the one sole way to reach the lightsome regions.

---

16   *Contra Haereses* V, xxxi, 1 (*PG* 7, 1208-1209).
17   *Cat. XIII*, 39 (*PG* 33, 819-820); *Cat. XIV*, 20 (*PG* 33, 849-850).

The victory of Christ on the cross was Adam's victory also. In the poem by Cirillonas (fourth century), speaking of the redemption and Christ's ascension, he says: "See, the conflict is ended, Adam has received the crown." [18]

According to Jewish Christian thought, the foot of the cross planted on Calvary went down into the underground grotto where Adam was buried and where the just awaited the redemption. Thus, by means of the cross, as if by a ladder, Christ brought Adam back into paradise after washing him with his blood flowing on our first father through the rent in the rock.

The skull at the foot of the cross.

This stream of mystic theological ideas had a great influence on religious art. The reason is to be sought in the very concrete expression of Jewish Christian theological concepts. It lent itself much more easily to art than the abstractions of the Gentile-Christians.

For our present purpose, we may remark that there are many representations of the crucifixion with a skull at the foot of the cross. In their detail, they are not always the same. Sometimes there is the skull alone, sometimes the crossed bones, and, in some examples, one can see a stream of blood flowing from the wounds of the Crucified, descending to mark the skull beneath with a cross. This can be viewed, for instance, in the mosaic picture of the crucifixion in the church of Dafni (Greece) dating back to the 11-12th century.

Another artist, not content with an allusion to Adam under Calvary by means of the skull, had pictured him in his tomb, praying with hands upraised towards the cross. In this connection, also, there is the famous crucifixion scene which can be studied in the miniature of a 12th century manuscript kept in the library of

18   Cirillonas, in *L'Orient Syrien* 10 (1965), 319.

Valenciennes, France. In another miniature, Adam is seated on his tomb at the foot of the cross, collecting in a chalice the blood which descends from the wounds of Christ crucified.

The same idea is expressed in two pictures from a Coptic church. In these, too, we can see the figure of a man under the cross awaiting resurrection. There is certainly question of Adam. In accord with the concrete Jewish Christian manner of expression, the redemption descends on him. [19]

The mystery of the death and resurrection of Christ taught the Judaeo-Christians that the humanity of Christ became glorious only after his descent into Še'ol. Passing from earth to heaven, it was completely transformed. According to the same teaching, the same flesh will become a vivifying spirit for all Christ's followers.

Profanations by pagans.

Hadrian's pagan profanation was, in some ways, like the mystic theological aura with which the Judaeo-Christians surrounded Calvary and Bethlehem. Yet, it was, in reality, the direct opposite. In the article referred to, Testa states that "from coins belonging to Aelia Capitolina, it is clear that the Venus adored on Calvary was Astarte-Nike, with a crown on the brow, with a sceptre in the left hand and a human bust in the right. We do not know what she was trampling with the left foot." [20]

The author explains that the crown has the shape of a fortified wall, that the bust is identified by some (such as Hill) as that of the emperor, by others as Adonis-Tammuz, and that similar coins found in other places in Palestine show Astarte with a river flowing under the feet.

---

19 I. Mancini, "Adamo sotto il Calvario," in *LTS* 41 (1965), 277-282.
20 E. Testa, "Le 'Grotte dei Misteri' giudeo-cristiane," in *LA* 14 (1963-1964), 116-117; 106-107.

Testa stresses that both pagans and local Christians must have been well acquainted with the myth of the descent of Inanna-Istar into *arallu* (regions beyond the grave). Parallel with this was the myth of Astarte descending victoriously into Hades to revive Adonis-Tammuz and to bring back life to earth. Again, according to mythology, the heavenly goddess (Urania) storms the walls of Ereškigal and, after being despoiled, puts her clothing back on. She quenches her thirst with the water which gives life and, after three days, rises from the *arallu* to realize her triumph, being proclaimed and honored as the goddess of vegetation.

Regarding the Holy Sepulchre, the statue of Jove erected there was aimed at profaning the mystery celebrated on the spot by Judaeo-Christians. This is how Testa explains it: "Again, from Aelia Capitolina coins, we see that the Jove worshipped in the city was the Jove-Serapis, identified with Osiris-Apis (Hesar-Hapi of the Egyptians). He held on leash Cerberus, the *Good God of the Dead.* On his return victorious from the netherworld, he was also called 'the first-born of the dead.' However, he was not a ghost but a real person resuscitated with flesh and bones. Therefore, he was also called 'the first-born of the living.' By means of a 'ladder' he went back from earth to heaven and became the Sun-god (*Hlios-Serapis*), the Adonis-Tammuz of the Semites." [21] In view of the profanation which was so sacrilegious and so well-planned, we can easily understand why the Judaeo-Christians kept aloof from these places. To frequent them would have seemed a kind of apostasy or, at least, a *communicatio in sacris* with the pagans.

The mystic grotto on Mount Olivet.

Testa continues with a description of another place deeply venerated by the Judaeo-Christians, the grotto of the Eleona on Mount

---

21 *Idem, art. cit.,* 117.

Olivet. It, too, was surrounded by them with the mystic aura which we have spoken of relative to Bethlehem and Calvary.

According to their theories of "descent" and "ascent," it represented the last stage of the "descent" of the glorified Christ, just as the grottos at Bethlehem and under Calvary were linked with the "descent" of the Christ who could still suffer. To complete the idea, we should add that the several "ascents" are associated with the mysteries of the death, resurrection and ascension localized on Calvary, in the Holy Sepulchre and on Mount Olivet.

Aoccroding to the Judaeo-Christians, it was in this grotto that Christ taught, not only the doctrines reported by the evangelists but also other secret teachings. There he would have admitted to the *Mysteries of the Kingdom* the few *elect* who were to establish the Church. There he returned after his resurrection. There he remained, instructing his disciples for a more or less extensive period — from forty days to twelve years, according to the different sects which existed amongst the Judaeo-Christians.

The apocrypha often mention the Mount of Olives. In the *History of Joseph* it is said that Jesus was on top of this mountain when he announced the death of his foster-father. According to the *Epistle of the Apostles,* it was on the same spot that Jesus initiated his disciples into fraternal charity. The *Ascension of Isaiah,* which describes the triumphal return of Christ into heaven, mentions the Mount of Olives in local reference. The *Transitus Mariae* has the Virgin praying there before being assumed into heaven. The *Gospel of Bartholomew* and the *Pistis Sophia* described the other events in the life of Jesus which took place on Mount Olivet. Later, when the Gentile Christians came, they built another shrine on Eleona commemorating especially the Eschatological Discourse (Matthew 24:1-44).

In the mystery of Christ's glorious ascension, the Judaeo-Christians substantially recalled the return of Jesus to glory, and his reception in the whole cosmic world (that in the heavens, on the earth and under the earth; cfr. Phil 2 :9f.), together with the consequent glorification of his faithful followers.

As is clear, the essence of this mystery is orthodox, but the outlook is expressed in a way proper to the Semitic mentality. In a sense, this mystic theological aura with which the Judaeo-Christians had surrounded the "mystic grottos" did open a way for Celsus' charge that they were practising a kind of Mystery Religion. Origen was not able to counter this completely. He confined himself to explaining it in the sense that the Christians availed themselves of the caves for religious purposes and restricted worship there to certain groups. "In his work, dreamed up against the Christians, Celsus mixes with his calumnies against them things which were never stated by them or, at least, by only a few, of whom none remain, or, at least, very few." [22]

2. *Results relative to ecumenism.*

The discoveries concerning the Judaeo-Christians are pertinent to matters of great practical import today. One such sphere is that of ecumenism. In this respect, the rediscovery of the Church of the Circumcision gives food for thought from two viewpoints : one, shall we say, negative; the other, positive.

From the negative angle, the discovery has made us aware of how the Judaeo-Christians began to decline when a new mentality and a new culture penetrated the Church. In other words, they started to disappear when what is called the "Great Church" began to make itself felt in Palestine. Their extinction was in sight when the new movement gained undisputed dominance. Its intolerance and its passion for unifying everything are the basic reasons for the decline. It meant, first, the recision or cutting off of the Judaeo-

---

22 *Contra Celsum* VI, 26 (*PG* 11, 1332).

Christians from the vital trunk of Christianity and, in the end, its total disappearance.

From the positive viewpoint, it would seem that the discoveries relative to the Church of the Circumcision are truly providential. It would be commonplace to stress the new spirit breathing through the Church at present, as a result of Vatican Council II with its directives on tolerance and respect for human values and the cultures of all peoples. The rediscovery has positive value for the apostolate. The Children of Israel can take note that, in the first centuries of Christianity, there was in existence a Jewish Christian Church with its own culture, language and spiritual values, grafted onto the teaching of Christ. It is once more possible to realize this, given the new spirit within the Church today, while, on the other hand, fear of losing one's own characteristics is no longer justified.

A booklet based on such considerations has recently appeared, written by Sofia Cavalletti.[23] She states summarily that, from the moment Jesus adopted Hebrew culture, spoke Hebrew, lived in a Hebrew environment and announced the Gospel to the Jews first of all, it would be absurd to reject what is good in Judaism in order to turn to other cultures further removed from the direct line of revelation. The writer evidently judges the present an opportune time to launch these ideas, now that we understand that the Graeco-Roman culture cannot of itself enfold and present the full Christian message to all peoples.

From this same ecumenical viewpoint, another contribution of the finds relative to the Church of the Circumcision is that it has solved the problem of the nature of the primitive Church of Palestine. This is a question which has been much debated in the past few years.

23   S. Cavalletti, *Ebraismo e spiritualità cristiana*. Rome, 1966.

Myriam Lemaire,[24] a Belgian who works amongst the Greek-Catholics in Jordan, writes in a report from Zerka: "The Christians are divided into various communities. The Greek-Catholics are the traditional Church of the East, going back directly to the apostles." The claim reflects a mentality which is widely known in the environment in which she lives. This conviction has urged its holders to take a hostile attitude towards the other communities who are regarded as intruders. Now the finds relative to the Church of the Circumcision have proven that it was really the primitive Church of Palestine, and that the Gentile-Christian Church was established in the Holy Land at a later date. This came about not without a certain arrogance at times: "by Constantine's orders" (*iussu Constantini*) as the Bordeaux Pilgrim put it, in 333, when speaking of the three basilicas built by that emperor. Thus, in our own time, the whole aspect of the problem is changed.

Actually, the fact that the Judaeo-Christians lived on in the villages, and in the main places of the redemption, all through the first centuries, with their own worship and traditions, puts all rites which subsequently appeared on the same juridical footing. It also allows us to foresee that, in future, that Church will remain in charge of the situation which shows that it possesses the greatest energy, fruitful in multiple activities.

24 M. Lemaire, in *La Missione*, Milan, 1966, no. 31, 125.

CONCLUSION

Ending this résumé of the finds and studies on Jewish Christianity, we can state that, with regard to the history of the Church in Palestine during the first four centuries, we are in possession of ideas which vary considerably from what was hitherto taken for granted. Here is an example of this latter.

"The revolt ended in a disaster. The destruction of the Jerusalem Temple and State, in 70, was a fatal blow for Jewish Christianity.... Goodbye to the prestige of the mother Church and its formulation of Jewish Christianity. Situated far from the great missionary roads and the major spiritual currents, isolated by reason of geographical position and their legalism, the Judaeo-Christians of Pella, genuine heirs of the apostolic group, ceased to count. Living on the margin of a Church which tended to become more and more that of the Gentiles, they would soon be reduced to the rank of an obscure heretical sect, the Ebionites and Nazarenes." With these words Marcel Simon ended his first volume on the first Christians.[1]

In place of all this, the new discoveries show that neither 70 nor 135 marked the end of the Church of Jewish origin, nor did those dates signify the full and undisputed spread of the "Great Church" or that of the Gentile-Christians. The statement by Simon is too cut and dried. In the greater part of Palestine, especially in the mountain areas, the Church of the Circumcision lived on quite actively to the end of the fourth century and then, in a state of

---

1   M. Simon, *Les premiers chrétiens*. Paris, 1960, p. 124.

decline, for another two centuries. The archaeological material proves that there existed side by side in the Holy Land (at least through the fourth and fifth centuries) the "Church of the Circumcision" and the "Church of the Gentiles."

Again, according to the new finds, the Church of the Circumcision had its own liturgy, expressive of Christian teaching with its roots in Judaism, with its own books, buildings, worship and customs. The discoveries also show that the neighbouring countries felt a considerable Jewish Christian influence, especially the Asia Minor of which the Apocalypse speaks.

Besides, studies on the Judaeo-Christians have thrown new light on the question of the antiquity of the Holy Places. In many cases, the documentation of the traditions allows us to trace them back to the beginning, thus bridging the gap through the period from the apostles to Constantine. One example is Nazareth. Ancient inscriptions and archaeological discoveries bear witness to Christian worship of Mary there already in the very first centuries.

Finally, these studies are very important for their contribution to a fuller and more exact understanding of certain New Testament passages, especially in the Apocalypse. There, the five elements of the Jewish Christian system of symbolism appear together.

In the beginning, the Church of the Gentiles was not the "Great Church" in Palestine, much less the dominant one. It formed simply a part of the Church of Christ which slowly became the only one after the Church of the Circumcision disappeared without leaving any deep traces.

Taking into account the results which are already scientifically proven, students of Church History, those interested in the development of Christian thought, specialists in sacred art (particularly those who study the long, but ever-vital re-application of architectural and iconographical elements which have become traditional) — all will find something with which to revive and round out their studies when dealing with Christian beginnings.

BIBLIOGRAPHY

W. F. Albright, Review of Gli scavi del "Dominus Flevit," by Bagatti-Milik in *Bulletin of the American Schools of Oriental Research* no. 159 (October, 1960) 37-38.

M. Avi-Yonah, Review of *GSDF* in *Israel Exploration Journal* 11 (1961) 91-94.

— In collaboration with M. W. Prausnitz and D. Barag, *Excavations at Shavei Zion*. Rome, 1967.

Bagatti, B., O.F.M., "Resti cristiani in Palestina anteriori a Costantino?" in *Rivista di Archeologia cristiana* 26 (1950) 117-131.

— "Scoperta di un cimitero giudeo-cristiano al 'Dominus Flevit' (Monte-Oliveto - Gerusalemme)" in *Liber Annuus* 3 (1952-1953) 149-184.

— "Il 'Min' Giacobbe in Kafar Soma delle fonti rabbiniche" in *La Terra Santa* 32 (1956) 170-171.

— "Nuovi elementi per spiegare l'origine della Croce cristiana" in *L'Osservatore Romano* (June 24, 1957, p. 3); and in Spanish in *La Tierra Santa*, 1957, pp. 341-346.

— "Kaukab. In questo paese vissero i parenti del Signore," in *La Terra Santa* 33 (1957) 140-143.

— *Gli scavi del "Dominus Flevit"* (*Monte Oliveto - Gerusalemme*). *Part I*: *La necropoli del periodo romano* (in collaboration with J. T. Milik for the inscriptions). Jerusalem, 1958. Pp. 191 and 44 Plates.

— "Una pagina inedita della Chiesa primitiva," in *L'Osservatore Romano* (August 6, 1960); and in *LTS* 36 (1960) 230-236. Preview of E. Testa's study of *Jewish-Christian* symbolism in *Il simbolismo dei Giudeo-cristiani*.

— "Ricerche su alcuni antichi siti giudeo-cristiani," in *LA* 11 (1960-1961) 288-314. (Mentioned are Kaukab, Kefer Simai, Kefer Sechanya, Jethira, Anea, Khirbet Kilkish, Bakatha, Koraiatha, houses of the Sampsei.)

— "Gezer cristiana," in *LTS* 37 (1961) 286--289.

— *L'Archeologia cristiana in Palestina*. Florence: Sansoni. Pp. 279 with 16 Plates. (The first chapter deals with pre-Constantine Palestine.)

— "Tracce giudeo-cristiane nella regione delle Sette Chiese dell'Apocalisse," in *LA* 12 (1961-1962), 177-220.

— "Le origini della 'tomba della Vergine' al Getsemani," in *Rivista Biblica* 11 (1963) 38-52.

— "Le idee dei sette cieli," in *LTS* 39 (1963) 8-10.

— "Gerusalemme e Betlemme negli antichi mosaici," in *LTS* 39 (1963) 101-105.

— "Antiche lucerne battesimali" in *LTS* 39 (1963) 165-168.

— "Giscala Cristiana," in *LTS* 39 (1963) 293-299.

— "Le origini delle tradizioni dei Luoghi Santi," in *LA* 14 ((1936-1946) 32-64.

— "Probabile figura del Precursore in un graffito di Nazaret," in *Oriens Antiquus* 3 (1964) 61-66.

— "Al centro degli Arcontici, Kh. Kilkish presso Hebron," in *LTS* 40 (1964) 264-269.

— *L'Eglise de la Circoncision*. Translated by A. Storme from the Italian manuscript. Jerusalem, 1965. Pp. vii- 286.

— "Ricerche su alcuni segni delle Catacombe romane," in *LA* 15 (1964-1965) 98-123.

— "Le antichità di Kh. Qana e di Kefr Kenna in Galilea," in *LA* 15 (1964-1965) 251-292.

— "Naim del Vangelo," in *LTS* 41 (1965) 10-19.

— "Ba'ineh, Villaggio Inghiottito," in *LTS* 41 (1965) 78-82.

— "Tradizione e arte a Shefa 'Amr in Galilea," in *LTS* 41 (1965) 180-187.

— "Tiberiade Paleocristiana," in *LTS* 42 (1966) 137-142.

— "Nuovi apporti archeologici sul pozzo di Giacobbe in Samaria," in *LA* 16 (1965-1966) 127-164. (Treatment of the Samaritan Christian Church.)

— "Il cristianesimo a Seforis in Galilea," in *LTS* 43 (1967) 3-9.

— "Alla ricerca della tomba del Min Giacobbe," in *LTS* 43 (1967) 74-77.

— *Gli scavi di Nazaret. Volume I: Dalle origini al secolo XII.* Jerusalem, 1967. Pp. vii-316 with 9 Plates. English translation: Eugene Hoade, *Excavations in Nazareth*. Jerusalem, 1969.

— *Luoghi santi e santuari di S. Pietro in Siria-Palestina* in *San Pietro*. Atti della XIX settimana biblica. Brescia, 1967, pp. 535-548.

— *L'Eglise de la gentilité en Palestine* (Ier-XI siècle). Adapted from the Italian manuscript by A. Storme. Jerusalem, 1968. Pp. viii-358.

— *La figura ed il martirio di S. Pietro secondo i giudeo-cristiani di Palestina*, in *Pietro e Paolo* nel XIX centenario del martirio. Naples, 1969. Pp. 169-179.

— *Le due redazioni del "Transistus Mariae"* in *Marianum* 32 (1970) 279-287.

D. Baldi, O.F.M., *Enchiridion Locorum Sanctorum*. 2nd ed. Jerusalem, 1955.

E. Beaucamp, O.F.M., Review of *ISGC* in *LA* 12 (1961-1962) 334-338.

P. Benoit, O.P., "La nouvelle église de l'Annonciation à Nazareth," in *La vie intellectuelle*, Juin, 1955, 26-28.

180

M. Canciani, Review of *LHF* in *L'Osservatore della Domenica*, September 30, 1967, p. 19.

S. Cavalletti, "Il 'sigillo di Dio," in *L'Osservatore Romano*, August 10, 1961, p. 5.

— *Ebraismo e spiritualità cristiana*. Rome, 1966. Pp. 201.

— Review of *LEC* in *Studi e materiali di Storia delle Religioni* 37 (1966) 125-128.

— "Segno, simbolo, tipo nell'ebraismo e nel cristianesimo primitivo" in *Il segno nella Liturgia*, Padova 1970, 41-61.

C. Cecchelli, *Il trionfo della Croce*. Rome, 1954. Pp. 62-63; 161-168.

C. Chelveder, O.F.M., "Symboles chrétiens au village des Pasteurs," in *La Terre Sainte*, 1964, pp. 224-226.

Ch. Clermont-Ganneau, "Épigraphes hébraïques et grecques sur des ossuaires juifs inédits," in *Revue Archéologique*, May-June, 1883, pp. 257-268. Also in *Archaeological Researches in Palestine during the Years* 1873-1874. London, 1899, pp. 381-412.

G. Concetti, O.F.M., "Gli scavi di Nazaret dalle origini al XII," in *L'Osservatore Romano*, Novembre 23, 1967. Review of Bagatti's book.

M. Conti, O.F.M., "Nuove scoperte a Nazaret," in *Bibbia e Oriente* 4 (1962) 17-19.

V. Corbo, O.F.M., "La casa del Principe degli Apostoli ritrovata a Cafarnao," in *L'Osservatore Romano*, June 29-30, 1968, p. 8.

— "La casa di S. Pietro a Cafarnao" in *LA* 18 (1968) 15-54.

— *The House of Saint Peter at Capharnaum*. Translated from the Italian by S. Saller. Jerusalem, 1969.

— *New Memoirs of Saint Peter by the Sea of Galilee*. Translated from the Italian by G. Bushell. Jerusalem, 1969.

I. H. Dalmais, O. P., Review of *LEC* in *Bible et Terre Sainte* No. 92 (1967), 23.

— Review of *Les symboles chrétiens primitifs* by Daniélou in *La vie spirituelle*, April, 1961, pp. 482-483.

J. Daniélou, S.J., *Théologie du Judéo-Christianisme*. Paris, 1958.

— *Les symboles chrétiens primitifs*. Paris 1961. English translation: *Primitive Christian Symbols*. London, 1964. (Illustrated by finds in Palestine.)

— Review of *ISGC*, *LEC* and of *LHF* in *Recherches de Sciences Religieuses* 51 (1963) 117-121; 55 (1967) 92-96 and 56 (1968) 119-120.

— *Pierre dans le Judéo-christianisme hétérodoxe* in *San Pietro*. Brescia, 1967, pp. 443-458.

— *That the Scripture might be fulfilled* and *The Word goes forth* in *The Crucibles of Christianity* by A. Toynbee, London 1969, pp. 261-298.

J A. De Aldama, S. J., Review of *ISGC* in *Estúdios Ecclesiásticos* 41 (1966) 579-580.

R. De Vaux, O.P., Review of *GSDF* in *RB* 66 (1959) 299-301.

L Diez Merino, "Origen de los signos que acompañan a las inscripciones nabateas del Sinai," in *LA* 19 (1969) 264-304.

O. Englebert. "Les franciscains et la grâce des lieux-saints," in *Evangile aujoud'hui* 57 (1968) 67-72. Review of Bagatti's *Gli scavi di Nazaret*.

T. Federici, "Il Simbolismo dei Giudeo-cristiani," in *L'Osservatore Romano,* January 21, 1965; also in *LTS* 41 (1965) 46-50.

Th. Frankfort, Review of *GSDF* in *Latomus* 20 (1961) 415-416.

C. Garbini, Review of *LEC* in *Oriens Antiquus* 5 (1966) 300-302.

A. Hamman, Review of *LEC* in *Mélanges de Science Religieuse* 23 (1966) 241-242.

A. Janssen, Review of *L'Huile de la Foi*, in *Ephemerides Theologicae Lovanienses* 43 (1967) 608.

C. Kopp, *Die heiligen Stätten der Evangelien*. Regensburg, 1959. Pp. 86-106.

R. Le Déaut, C.S.Sp., "La symbolique judéo-chrétienne," in *Biblica* 47 (1966) 283-289.

G. Lomiento, Review of *ISGC* in *Vetera christianorum* 1 (1964) 167-170.

I. Mancini, O.F.M., "Preghiere eucaristiche dei giudeo-cristiani," in *LTS* 40 (1964) 355-358.

— "La 'Ecclesia ex circumcisione'," in *Bibbia e Oriente* 7 (1965) 77-87.

— "Un artista cristiano nella sinagoga di Dura-Europos," in *LTS* 41 (1965) 171-174.

— "Adamo sotto il Calvario," in *LTS* 41 (1965) 277-282.

— "Un aspetto della teologia giudeo-cristiana: Cristo Angelo," in *LTS* 42 (1966) 72-76.

J. T. Milik, "Une amulette judéo-araméenne," in *Biblica* 48 (1967) 450-451.

L. Moraldi, "Nuova luce sui giudeo-cristiani in un libro recente," in *Rivista Biblica* 11 (1963) 196-205. (The article deals with Testa's *Il simbolismo dei Giudeo-cristiani*.)

R. Motte, O.M.I., "Ossuaries," in *Dictionnaire de la Bible — Supplément* 6, coll. 945-946.

R. North, S.J., Review of *ISGC* in *The Catholic Biblical Quarterly* 24 (1962) 441-443; also of *Gli scavi di Nazaret*, in *Biblica* 49 (1968) 171-173.

L.-M. Orrieux, Review of *ISGC, LEC* and *LHF* in *Lumière et vie* 16 (1967) 113-115; 17 (1968) 122.

A. Parrot, *Golgotha et Saint-Sépulchre*. Paris 1955, pp. 92-93.

182

A Penna, C.R.I., Review of *Gli scavi di Nazaret* by Bagatti in *Rivista Biblica* 15 (1967) 441-444.

J -C. Picard. "L'Huile de la Foi," in *La Terre Sainte* 1967, pp. 150-152. Italian translation in *LTS* 43 (1967) 131-135.

J B. Pritchard, Review of *GSDF* in *American Journal of Archaeology* 64 (1960) 302.

G. Rainoldi, "Alle origini della Chiesa," in *L'Italia* November 3, 1965, p. 3 (Review of *LEC*).

L Randellini, O.F.M., Review of Bagatti's "Resti cristiani in Palestina anteriori a Costantino?" in *Palestra del Clero* 30 (1951) 1183-1184.

— "La Chiesa della Circoncisione e la sua storia," in *Studi Francescani* 64 (1967) 3-47. Printed separately as *La Chiesa dei Giudeo-cristiani*. Brescia, 1968. Pp. 72.

E. Ravarotto, O.F.M., Review of *GSDF* in *Antonianum* 34 (1968) 345-347.

A. Recio, O.F.M., Review of *Gli scavi di Nazaret* in *Antonianum* 40 (1968) 335-337.

G. Rinaldi, C.R.S., "Scoperte archeologiche a Gerusalemme," in *L'Osservatore Romano*, August 14, 1958. (Review of *GSDF*.)

— Notes on *ISGC* and on *LEC* in *Bibbia e Oriente* 5 (1963) 79-80; 7 (1965) 263-264.

— "Giacomo, Paolo e i Giudei (Atti 21, 17-26)," in *Rivista Biblica* 14 (1966) 407-423.

A. Rolla, "Notiziario archeologico palastinese," in *Rivista Biblica* 11 (1963) 58-59. (Notes on the Nazareth excavations.)

S. Saller, O.F.M., "The Archaeological Setting of the Shrine of Bethphage," in *LA* 11 (1960-1961) 172-250; Volume I of *Collectio Minor* of the Studium Biblicum Franciscanum.

— "Sepulchral Scoops," in *Around the Province*, pp. 110-112.

N. Séd, "Hymnes sur le Paradis de Saint-Ephrem et les traditions juives," in *Le Muséon LXXXI* (1968) 492, relative to no. 888.

Ph. Seidensticker, O.F.M., "Ein judenchristlicher Friedhof aus apostolischer Zeit." in *Franziskanische Studien* 40 (1958) 405-412.

— "Ein Friedhof der Urgemeinde von Jerusalem entdecker?" in *Bible und Kirche* 14 (1959). 13-19.

— "Gräber der Urkirche," in *Echo der Zeit*, March 1, 1959, p. 16. (Dealing with *GSDF*.)

— Review of *LEC* in *Franziskanische Studien* 48 (1966) 180-181.

J. Starcky, Review of *LHF* in *RB* 75 (1968) 278-280.

A. Storme, "L'Eglise de la circoncision d'après les fouilles récentes," in *The Australian Journal of Archaeology* 1 (1968) 29-40.

E. L. Sukenik, "The Earliest Records of Christianity," in *American Journal of Archaeology* 51 (1947) 351-365; abbreviated and modified in *Atti del I Congresso Nazionale di Archeologia cristiana*. Rome, 1952. Pp. 267-268.

M. Tagliacozzo, Review of *ISGC* in *La Rassegna mensile di Israele* 34 (1968) 297-299.

— Review of *LEC* in *La Rassegna mensile di Israele* 35 (1969) 49-50.

J. L. Teicher, "Ancient Eucharistic Prayers in Hebrew," in *The Jewish Quarterly Review* 54 (1963-1964), 99-109.

E. Testa, O.F.M., *Gesù pacificatore universale*. S. Maria degli Angeli. 1956. Pp. 182. (The angels and Jewish Christian teaching; cfr. Lemaire in *LA* 7 (1956-1957) 283-286.

— "La 'Gerusalemme celeste': dall'Antico Oriente alla Bibbia e alla Liturgia," in *Bibbia e Oriente* 1 (1959) 47-50.

— "Fruttuose ricerche archeologiche palestinesi," in *L'Osservatore Romano*, September 25, 1960, p. 3.

— "Il rito battesimale nella Chiesa madre," in *Bibbia e Oriente* 2 (1960) 54-57.

— "De symbolismo ecclesiae matris," in *Verbum Domini* 39 (1961) 141-161.

— "The Graffiti of Tomb 21 at Bethphage," in *LA* 11 (1960-1961) 251-287.

— *Il simbolismo dei Giudeo-cristiani*. Jerusalem, 1962. Pp. xxxii-590 and 47 Plates.

— "Spiritualità della Chiesa di Giacomo," in *S. Giacomo il Minore*. Jerusalem, 1962, pp. 35-51. French translation, *Saint Jacques le Mineur*, pp. 36-49.

— "Le Grotte mistiche dei Nazareni e i loro riti battesimali," In *LA* 12 (1961-1962) 5-45.

— "L'uso degli Ossuari tra i monaci di Siria," In *LTS* 39 (1963) 36-41.

— "Scoperta del Primitivo Rito della Estrema Unzione in una Laminella del I secolo," in *LTS* 39 (1963) 70-74; *L'Osservatore Romano*, February 8, 1963.

— "I proseliti giudeo-cristiani," in *LTS* 39 (1963) 132-138.

— "Influssi giudeo-cristiani nei monasteri di San Pacomio," in *LTS* 39 (1963) 330-335. (Medieval graffiti.)

— "Abbiamo visto la sua stella in Oriente (Matt. 2,2)," in *LTS* 40 (1964) 11-18.

— "La Piscina Probatica, monumento pagano o giudaico?" in *LTS* 40 (1964) 311-316. (Jewish Christian tradition.)

184

— "Le 'Grotte dei Misteri' giudeo-cristiane," in *LA* 14 (1963-1964), 65-144. Presented with changes in *Il Messianismo*. Atti della XVIII Settimana Biblica a cura dell'A.B.I. Brescia, 1966, pp. 331-355.

— "Le Cene del Signore," in *LTS* 41 (1965) 116-121.

— "Il Paradiso a Nazaret," in *LTS* 41 (1965) 265-271.

— "La creazione del mondo nel pensiero dei SS. Padri (Contributo alla storia della esegesi)," in *LA* 16 (1965-1966), 5-68. (Pages 5-21 deal with the symbolic exegesis of the Judaeo-Christians.)

— "La diffusione della chiesa Giudeo-cristiana," in *LTS* 42 (1966) 100-105.

— "Nuove scoperte a Nazaret," in *LTS* 42 (1966) 308-312. (Finding of a statue of St. Peter and medieval graffiti.

— "Due frammenti di Targum sull'Incarnazione scoperti a Nazaret," in *LTS* 43 (1967) 99-104.

— "Il Targum di Isaia 55, 1.13, scoperto a Nazaret e la Teologia sui pozzi dell'Acqua Viva," in *LA* 17 (1967) 259-289.

— "Il 'Sigillo di Jahve'" in *Bibbia e Oriente* 9 (1967) 39-42.

— *L'Huile de la Foi. L'Onction des malades sur une lamelle du Ier siècle.* Traduit et adapté de l'italien par O. Englebert. Jerusalem, 1967. Pp. 136.

— "S. Pietro nel pensiero dei giudeo-cristiani," in *San Pietro*. Brescia, 1967, pp. 459-500.

— "Una Falsificazione della Laminella dell'Unzione," in *LTS* 44 (1968), 55-58.

— "Ancora sulla laminella giudeo-cristiana," in *Biblica* 49 (1968) 249-253.

— "L'apporto delle iscrizioni nazaretane," in *Rivista Biblica* 16 (1968) 167-185.

— "Il Paradiso dell'Eden secondo i SS. Padri," in *LA* 18 (1968) 94-152. (Exegesis of the Judaeo-Christians).

— "Genesi, Introduzione, Storia primitiva," in *La Sacra Bibbia*. Turin, 1969.

— *Nazaret Giudeo-cristiana*. Riti, Iscrizioni, Simboli. Jerusalem, 1969. Pp. 145.

— *Il peccato di Adamo nella patristica*. Jerusalem 1970. Pp. XIII-217.

— La figura di Noè secondo i Padri", in *LA* 20 (1970 138-144 (Exegesis of the Judaeo-Christians).

P. Testini, Review of *GSDF* in *Rivista di Archeologia cristiana* 35 (1959) 250-253.

J. Van Der Ploeg, O.P., Review of *GSDF* in *Journal of Semitic Studies* 5 (1960) 81-82.

F. Vattioni, Review of *GSDF* in *Rivista Biblica* 7 (1959) 81-83.

V. Vilar Hueso, "Onomastica neotestamentaria y símbolos cristianos en el cemeterio de 'Dominus Flevit'," in *Estúdios Biblicos* 18 (1959) 285-291.

F. Uricchio, O.F.M. Conv., Review of *LEC* in *Miscellanea Franciscana* 67 (1967) 213-215.

E. Vogt, S.J., "Sepulcra christiana I saec. in Monte Olivarum?" in *Biblica* 35 (1954) 274.

S. Voigt, O.F.M., "Nossa Capa," in Ioâo Batista by J. Daniélou. Petropolis, 1965, pp. 139-141. (Nazareth Graffiti.)

INDEX OF NAMES

INDEX OF SUBJECTS

194

LIST OF ILLUSTRATIONS

Page

PUBLICATIONS

OF THE STUDIUM BIBLICUM FRANCISCANUM

Collectio Maior

No. 1. *The Memorial of Moses on Mount Nebo*: Part I (Text) $ 9.00
and Part II (Plates) by S. SALLER, Jerusalem, 1941; 6.75
Part III (The Pottery) by H. SCHNEIDER, Jerusalem, 1950. 6.75

No. 2. FRA NICCOLO DA POGGIBONSI, O.F.M., *Libro d'Oltramare*:
The Italian Text of A. BACCHI revised and annotated by
B. BAGATTI. 6.75

English translation (*A Voyage beyond the Seas*) by
T. BELLORINI and E. HOADE, Jerusalem, 1945. 6.75

No. 3. S. SALLER, *Discoveries at St. John's, 'Ein Kârim, 1941-2,*
Jerusalem, 1946. 6.75

No. 4. B. BAGATTI, *I Monumenti di Emmaus el-Qubeibeh e dei
Dintorni,* Jerusalem, 1947. 6.75

No. 5. B. BAGATTI, *Il Santuario della Visitazione ad 'Ain Kârim
(Montana Judaeae),* Jerusalem, 1948. 6.75

No. 6. FRESCOBALDI, GUCCI and SIGOLI, *Visit to the Holy Places
of Egypt, Sinai, Palestine and Syria in* 1384, translated
from the Italian by T. BELLORINI and E. HOADE, with a
Preface and Notes by B. BAGATTI, Jerusalem, 1948. 6.75

No. 7. S. SALLER and B. BAGATTI, *The Town of Nebo (Khirbet
El-Mekhayat), with a Brief Survey of other Ancient
Christian Monuments in Transjordan,* Jerusalem, 1949. 8.25

No. 8. FRA FRANCESCO SURIANO, *Treatise on the Holy Land,*
translated from the Italian by T. BELLORINI and E. HOADE,
with a Preface and Notes by B. BAGATTI, Jerusalem, 1948. 6.75

No. 9. B. BAGATTI, *Gli antichi edifici sacri di Betlemme,* Jerusalem,
1952. 8.25

No. 10.   Fra Bernardino Amico, *Plan of the Sacred Edifices of the Holy Land*, translated from Italian by T. Bellorini and E. Hoade, with a Preface and Notes by B. Bagatti, Jerusalem, 1953.   6.75

No. 11.   V. Corbo, *Gli scavi di Khirbet Siyar el-Ghanam (Campo dei Pastori) e i monasteri dei dintorni*, Jerusalem, 1955.   6.75

No. 12.   S. Saller, *Excavations at Bethany* (1949-1953), Jerusalem, 1957.   18.00

No. 13.   B. Bagatti e J. T. Milik, *Gli scavi del "Dominus Flevit" (Monte Oliveto — Gerusalemme)*, 1 Parte: La necropoli del periodo romano, Jerusalem, 1958.   6.75

          Part II : S. J. Saller, *The Jebusite Burial Place*, Jerusalem, 1964.   10.50

No. 14.   P. E. Testa, *Il Simbolismo dei Giudeo - Cristiani*, Jerusalem, 1962.   25.50

No. 15.   Fr. Elzear Horn, *Ichnographiae Monumentorum Terrae Sanctae* (1724-1744), translated from Latin by E. Hoade, with preface by B. Bagatti, Jerusalem, 1962.   9.00

No. 16.   V. Corbo, *Ricerche Archeologiche al Monte degli Ulivi*, Jerusalem, 1965.   10.50

No. 17.   B. Bagatti, *Gli Scavi di Nazaret*, Jerusalem, 1967.   12.00

          English translation (*Excavations in Nazareth*) by E. Hoade, Jerusalem, 1969.   12.00

No. 18.   E. Hoade, *Western Pilgrims*, Jerusalem, 1970.   4.00

Collectio Minor

No. 1.   S. J. Saller and E. Testa, *The Archaeological Setting of the Shrine of Bethphage*, Jerusalem, 1961.   1.50

No. 2.   B. Bagatti, *L'Église de la Circoncision*, Jérusalem, 1965   6.75

No. 3.   P. E. Testa, *L'Huile de la Foi*, (L'Onction des malades sur une lamelle du Ier siècle), Jérusalem, 1967.   2.25

No. 4.   B. Bagatti, *L'Église de la gentilité en Palestine* (Ier-XIe siècle), Jérusalem, 1968.   7.00

No. 5.   V. CORBO. *The House of St. Peter at Capharnaum, Translated by* S. SALLER, Jerusalem, 1969.   2.00

No. 6.   S. SALLER, *A Revised Catalogue of the Ancient Synagogues of the Holy Land,* Jerusalem, 1969.   2.00

No. 7.   S. LOFFREDA, *Scavi di Et-Tabgha* (*Lago di Tiberiade*), Gerusalemme   1970.   3.00

No. 8.   E. TESTA, *Nazaret Giudeo-Cristiana. Riti. Iscrizioni. Simboli.* Gerusalemme 1969.   2.00

No. 9.   V. CORBO, ST. LOFFREDA, A. SPIJKERMAN, *La Sinagoga di Cafarnao,* Gerusalemme 1970.   2.00

Analecta

No. 1.   A. LANCELLOTTI, *Grammatica della Lingua Accadica.* Jerusalem, 1962.   9.00

No. 2.   M. MIGUENS, *El Paraclito* (Jn 14-16), Jerusalem, 1963.   4.50

No. 3.   P. E. TESTA, *Il Peccato di Adamo nella Patristica* (*Gen. III*), Gerusalemme, 1970.   3.50

LIBER ANNUUS

I - XIV   Out of print.

Vol. XV   (1964-65) 6.00

Vol. XVI   (1965-66) 8.00

Vol. XVII   (1967) 8.00

Vol. XVIII   (1968) 8.00

Vol. XIX   (1969) 9.00

Vol. XX   (1970) 9.00

Obtainable from:

Franciscan Printing Press
P.O.B. 186
Jerusalem,
Israel.

Centro Propaganda e Stampa
di Terra Santa
V. Gherardini, 7
20145 - Milano, Italia.

The Prices are quoted in U.S.A. dollars;

they do not include the cost of shipping.